Prepping

Natural Disasters, Nuclear Wars and the End of the World

(An Essential Survival Guide for Diy Preppers Who Want to Be Self-reliant)

Keith Brock

Published By **Zoe Lawson**

Keith Brock

Prepping: Natural Disasters, Nuclear Wars and the End of the World (An Essential Survival Guide for Diy Preppers Who Want to Be Self-reliant)

ISBN   978-1-998038-02-2

No part of this guidebook shall be reproduced in any form without permission in writing from the publisher except in the case of brief quotations embodied in critical articles or reviews.

Legal & Disclaimer

The information contained in this book is not designed to replace or take the place of any form of medicine or professional medical advice. The information in this book has been provided for educational & entertainment purposes only.

The information contained in this book has been compiled from sources deemed reliable, and it is accurate to the best of the Author's knowledge; however, the Author cannot guarantee its accuracy and validity and cannot be held liable for any errors or omissions. Changes are periodically made to this book. You must consult your doctor or get professional medical advice before using any of the suggested remedies, techniques, or information in this book.

Table Of Contents

Chapter 1: Why Prepare?

Whether you prepared for it or known as it nonsense, we're all glad that the area didn't cease, because the Ancient Mayans said it might, in 2012. That being stated, we are not off the hook as we may want to still face some screw ups in the destiny.

Tornadoes and hurricanes need to come into city and in reality hurricane your existence, or allow's say Country A invades Country B for supposedly humanitarian functions. Shhhh, don't inform. Armed soldiers are on the doorstep looking for some issue you don't have, and out of frustration, they without a doubt bomb your own home. The identical area whose mortgage you haven't even truely paid off but. Next thing , you grow to be roaming the streets. Maybe the monetary device ought to plummet on one dreadful night time, and tomorrow, hundreds of masses of people all over the global emerge as jobless.

What then? Well, you want to put together even in advance than all the ones misfortunes need to occur. You need to make certain that you have get proper of entry to to number one requirements in case you need to stay on. This ebook will guide you thru what you want to have accessible for terrific situations.

Let's start with why you want to put together for the opportunities of natural failures, wars, and economic turmoil. You may additionally moreover inquire from me, isn't that an excessive amount of horrible wondering? Can't we really stay as glass-1/2 of of-entire sort of humans and anticipate that now not some thing as drastic as tsunamis wiping off an entire coastal metropolis may additionally need to arise?

No. Review your information and inform me that sports like volcanic eruptions, devastating hurricanes, excessive worldwide financial crises, and global wars don't appear. You can't. Catastrophic events are an unlucky danger of human existence. Or in all likelihood, couldn't you clearly prepare after an statement regarding, allow's say, an incoming storm has been launched? No. Just no. Waiting till the closing hour to plan for a disaster isn't enough planning.

Suppose you're residing in a rustic wherein nearly now not something ever takes area, right for you. But there are others to be had whose nations enjoy twenty typhoons a 365 days or fifty earthquake shocks annually. Even if natural catastrophes aren't the standard headlines on your nearby newspaper, the fact that it isn't unthinkable need to provide you a clue that it is able to thoroughly take place to you too.

One day, your city can be in a country of emergency because of the fact the volcano mendacity dormant nearby has ultimately woken up. And in this case, you can discover the phrase consolation within the dictionary however nowhere else in real existence. The current era which you have come to depend on? The 24/7 keep two blocks away that's typically your looking floor whenever you're inside the temper for some Toblerone? I'm sorry, but you could kiss them goodbye and leave out them like hell.

Nowadays, we've come to rely considerably on what's on the spot and reachable. We have left out the pursuit of know-how and independence for the sake of consolation and instant gratification. We twist a knob at the range, and voila, a fireplace appears earlier than our eyes. We choose up our telephones, and pizza is on the doorstep half of an hour later. Admit it. We can't carry out clean each day sports activities with out the assist of electricity, immediately meals, and on foot water. Do you recognize a way to start a hearth with sincerely matchsticks and wood? Do you comprehend the manner to prepare meals that wasn't sealed in a can or displayed in a few fancy packaging?

You need to discover ways to do these things due to the fact the time will come whilst the ones capabilities might be wanted, and if you're now not prepared beforehand, you'll be the primary to go through or, worse, to die.

The hassle is, maximum humans are misinformed and uneducated approximately emergency preparations. Not super can we stay clueless about the right sports in case of sudden disasters, however we're moreover ambivalent approximately the trouble of mastering and coaching ourselves. What we have were given were given now might not continuously be there.

Prepping is vital because of the truth if there's one hassle hurricanes like Katrina and Sandy have taught us, it's that nature is a complain, and it doesn't play favorites. Poor or wealthy, you can emerge as lining for rations of meals and water. It doesn't depend in case you're the prettiest female in town. You may additionally need to need to go through no longer showering for every week due to the truth water can be scarce.

You don't get a say about your chances of being a sufferer of conditions, however you may do something quality approximately your survival skills if catastrophe does strike.

Chapter 2: What Is Prepping?

Prepping isn't always a fad, nor is it a

completely unique mission. Generations earlier than, it grow to be a fashionable exercise for each family to put together for worst-case situations. Pantries were stocked with meals, and cabinets were full of materials and distinctive critical devices. It changed into handiest even as people grew greater depending at the technology and services of different people that this workout have become unusual. Moreover, our developing expectation that the government can provide us with something we demand involves a faulty abandonment of self-reliance and independence.

Prepping is easy. Contrary to popular belief, it doesn't name for that you make investments all of your time, coins, and attempt in ensuring which you are bulletproof. It doesn't advise which you want to spend every single 2d of your life fretting over an coming near disaster. Instead, it's far about taking component on your existence as it is these days at the identical time as you prepare for what should possibly come the next day.

The commonplace idea humans have of preppers is that they're paranoid, tinfoil hat-carrying those who create bunkers full of factors. In fact, there are one-of-a-kind ranges. It can range from most effective a easy survival-package training to finish-out bunker creation, that is normally what laypeople had in mind whilst deliberating prepping. No depend quantity what degree of prepping you're inclined to adopt, it's far a given which you'll gain from a couple of distinct benefits prepping can offer you in case of an emergency.

Prepping works at the concept that if ever an emergency is stated, humans will rush out of their houses, honestly like there was no day after today, in the direction of the closest grocery and hardware shops to inventory up on smooth necessities. But there may be best a lot inventory a shop can provide, and on the prevent of the day, shelves may be emptied, and others will have not anything to carry home because of the truth demand obtained't healthful supply in instances like this. As a prepper, why are you better off?

For one, if you're already stocked in advance with what you want to live to inform the story, you gained't have to fear about speeding with different humans anymore to get your fingers first on fundamental necessities and hazard getting your self trampled.

Furthermore, in times while there may be no caution the least bit and the calamity actions, you can rest confident which you have what you want even though stores and clinical centers aren't to be had to you. You don't want to waste some time and strength stopping with others over the last can of red meat and beans, and as an alternative, you may interest your power on distinctive crucial obligations which you need to do.

The bottom line is, prepping is a form of mind-set. It is about assuming responsibility for one's personal welfare and independence from others. It moreover advocates self-sufficiency. People who shy away from making ready for disasters live within the faux assumption that necessities will generally be furnished to them through the authorities. They live their lives in comfort, and they'll be inclined to be lax due to the truth they may be so relying at the notion that assist will honestly come their manner.

Chapter 3: What Should You And Shouldn't Expect?

To stay on sooner or later of any type of disaster whether or not natural or guy-made, there are a few topics that you want to be aware about. Not identifying some statistics could be of a awesome disadvantage for you, so it'll possibly be better to preserve in thoughts the following:

1.Expect that public utilities may be closed down and will fail to art work.

Water, strength, communications, amongst others, received't be yours for the taking. Usually, the deliver or company to those number one goals is probably lessen off within the path of this time, and bulletins concerning at the identical time as they may be have end up once more on might not be to be had any time fast.

2.Expect that meals will no longer be on store cabinets.

Once facts about an incoming catastrophe has been disseminated, human beings will run like hell to the nearest shop and purchase the entirety they may. Even at some stage in calamities without caution, anticipate that a surge of humans can be competing inside the course of every different over a bottle of water. Food will run out speedy, and if you're no longer organized ahead, you could find nothing on the show shelves.

three.Expect that people will combat over the easy necessities.

One of the blessings of having equipped beforehand of time can be escaping this debacle. Calamities are decided times that might call for determined measures. You can't assume order in an occasion at the same time because the survival of an man or woman and their family may be the topmost precedence. Grocery stores might be the degree of the exceptional fights ever, and there's no longer whatever you can do approximately that. People can also combat over what they need to live on.

four.Expect the worst.

In any form of catastrophe, you need to bear in mind the worst-case conditions that could take location and prepare for them. You can normally desire for the super, however prepping is higher accomplished even as your mindset is hinged on all the necessities so that you can live on may be hard to get right of entry to. This manner, the immediate catastrophe actions, you are nicely-equipped and ready to respond due to this.

5.Don't count on for the government to address your non-public problems.

If you have got were given problem getting the government to pay interest your issues on a widespread day, what are the possibilities that they'll attend on your desires rapid during a catastrophe in particular whilst many humans are affected? It is probable that they may want time if you want to ship help for all and sundry. This is precisely why prepping intently emphasizes on self-reliance and independence.

You can't expect any device to be there for you and answer all of your issues. In times such as large calamities, there are loads of thousands of people that need interest. If you need to live to tell the tale, you better do something about it yourself in place of awaiting exclusive humans to head back and rescue you.

Part 2

Food Prepping for Everyone

Chapter 4: Food Prepping

Sorry, man. Most in all likelihood, you

acquired't be able to tell your mom to cook dinner dinner you her extremely good pancakes and purchase you Snickers inside the midnight on the nearest 7/eleven keep. In instances of catastrophe, you want to make do with what's available round you.

During natural catastrophes and emergencies, human beings typically react with fear and panic. They will go to shops and smooth the shelves of each canned food that they will don't forget. This is a first-rate bypass thinking about that in spite of the truth that the chance doesn't display up, people might likely although have a stock of food to be had for their households for the times to come back lower back back. But as a prepper, you could have a greater severa desire of meals. It lets in you to plot and thoroughly pick the meals you want due to the reality you aren't rushing to shop for things. Plus, whilst others are going crazy over on the cashier, you're no longer missing whatever as you do not forget final-minute problems like making sure your own family is nicely-knowledgeable and equipped about some component's coming.

The preferred idea of meals prepping is stocking up on food which can final for an extended duration and might keep you for months, if essential. Food is critical, as three weeks with out them may be fatal. So, you want to make sure that your pantry has enough supply.

Buy food that doesn't want refrigeration, which include canned meat, veggies, and tuna. It may additionally be appropriate to have sugar, tea, rice, bread, oil, powdered milk, and pasta, amongst others. Look out for profits inside the shops close by and buy bulks of products at lesser costs.

You would despite the fact that want cooking in some times, due to this which you need water and gasoline to cook dinner dinner your meals, like rice and straight away noodles.

Freeze-dried food and Meal Ready-to-Eat (additionally known as MRE) are also a number of your super options. They come in sealed packages which is probably geared up for instant eating. Designed for the navy, MREs are the last straight away food, as you'll simplest need to warm temperature them for a few minutes before they're prepared for consumption.

When talking about shelf-lifestyles, freeze-dried food can also have spherical ten to 20 years as compared to MREs that handiest have 3 to 5 years of shelf lifestyles. Freeze-dried meals is, therefore, better given that they wouldn't require opportunity. However, in case you however need to keep in thoughts searching for MREs for your survival meals garage, include them in your brief or medium-time period storage and replace them sometimes.

Chapter 5: Food Stockpiling

Determining what to buy can be mind-boggling, for the motive that there are lots

of food picks to be had. The extraordinary path of movement can be to stockpile food that is dense in nutrients. Avoid making an investment in chips and excellent food sorts that don't certainly hold dietary price. There is not any excuse for compromising your health, and cans of tuna and preserved greens must serve you a lot higher than 10 luggage of chips.

The secret is to attention on what you need in desire to what you want. If you're clamoring for snacks or chocolates, circulate for protein bars and chocolates. Chocolates, dark ones, in particular, can offer you with a short deliver of strength and one-of-a-type advantages. Plus, they don't absorb too much vicinity.

The next step in stockpiling is actually building it. This thing can unnerve a few human beings, and that they clamor to buy 100 cans of pork and beans unexpectedly. Don't get earlier of your self. You don't want to buy all one hundred cans in one buy. And a hundred may be an excessive amount of in case you're most effective prepping for yourself. Take an accurate and sincere assessment of your wishes and base your alternatives on that evaluation. Plan out your food. You can restriction the quantity of food you buy for a meal based totally on the energy or base it on serving sizes.

After making plans and whenever you're grocery shopping for, double the devices that you generally purchase, particularly the non-perishable ones; permit us to say that you commonly buy four cans of pork and beans; make it eight. This way, you'll be constructing your stockpile speedy.

Once you've got your stockpile sitting to your shelves, ensure that they do no longer bypass the expiration date. If no disaster has hit, devour a few thing out of your supply to avoid waste. Rotate and update your stock and normally located the present day devices you have supplied in the lower lower back without a doubt so what you operate are the ones you have sold first.

Another important phrase to maintain in mind is to buy food that you can manipulate to pay for. Do no longer push your economic limits via manner of purchasing 8 cans of red meat and beans whilst your wallet can't stretch a protracted way sufficient. Also, if you're prepping for others (e.G., circle of relatives people), you have to consider their options.

It is likewise encouraged to inventory a large shape of meals that offers each vitamins and satisfaction to avoid food fatigue. Avoid stocking up on only one form of meals because eventually, you could now not be able to belly ingesting the same kind of food again and again again, and it might just visit waste. Another drawback of consuming only one shape of meals is that it may lack a few nutrients that are wished through the frame.

Chapter 6: Cooking Food Without Power

There will generally be a higher chance of having a energy outage in some unspecified time in the destiny of disasters, so don't depend too much on energy on the same time as cooking. There are possibility techniques to put together dinner food; listed underneath are definitely some of them:

1.Open fireplace

This method can be tough, and it takes a few exercising to acquire cooking with an open hearth. However, that is the most commonplace opportunity warmth deliver for cooking food and might produce top notch outcomes while done nicely. You want to have quite some wood to maintain an open fireplace going. Kettles, iron skillets, and Dutch ovens, amongst others, may be applied to prepare dinner pretty a good deal a few issue that you'd want to over an open flame.

2.Volcano stoves

Volcano stoves can be an extraordinary opportunity to regular stovetop because they are very with out trouble saved as they may be collapsible. Furthermore, volcano stoves use 3 precise sorts of fuel. Namely wood, charcoal, and propane, so that you're now not constrained to truly one gas type. The performance of volcano stoves in terms of cooking meals is a few thing to be lauded at as nicely.

three.Grills

If you have got were given the choice of staying at home and aren't forced to stay at the streets, you may but lease your BBQ grill to prepare dinner your food. Just ensure that you moreover might also additionally have handy the vital gas (e.G., wood, charcoal, propane). The problem with grills is that some are not transportable, so if you need to transport a protracted manner from your house, you may't deliver it with you, and also you'd ought to research some different approach of cooking meals without energy.

4.Camp stoves

Suppose you've were given a camp variety mendacity spherical, then pinnacle! But you can't use them interior your steady haven, and you may want to stock up on gasoline (i.E., propane). Propane bottles generally closing spherical certainly an hour, so that you'd have troubles with garage and charge.

five.Stove-in-a-can

A variety-in-a-can is a transportable and light-weight device that you may consist of in your emergency kit. It is substantially cheaper, and it runs on replaceable compressed gasoline cells with an extended burning life.

6.Rocket stoves

Learning the way to cook dinner on rocket stoves is significantly smooth. This opportunity cooking tool runs on a wood-burning, excessive-temperature combustion chamber where warm temperature shoots out in the direction of your meals. An advantage a rocket variety has over the others is its severe overall performance. However, you want you bought a deliver of wood for fuel, and it's no longer that portable.

Part three

Water Prepping

Chapter 7: Sources Of Water

Water is a as an alternative underrated necessity. A lot of human beings typically determine upon one-of-a-kind kinds of drinks. But while catastrophe comes, water may be more liked than ever.

At gift, you will possibly anticipate it is in greater, however in fact, specially in situations like a disaster, water can turn out to be so confined that people grow to be with none get admission to to a deliver. Unless you live close to a frame of clean water (e.G., river, lake), finding a sufficient amount that would final you for months may be a difficult feat.

Wars – specially fundamental ones – aren't with out hassle resolved. After herbal disasters, it may take a big quantity of time earlier than offerings inside the organizations can run yet again. Every day can be a awful day, and you'll in no way understand while subjects can be robust once more.

At a few component, you may run out of substances, certainly one of which you could't stay without. Water is a critical necessity for human lifestyles. Therefore, the shortage of it need to no longer be disregarded as trivial. This segment will talk how you can find out unique water property even as the time comes the water you've got saved has all been depleted.

1.Rainwater

Make use of rainwater as it is able to be a deliver of potable water. You can use basins or buckets to seize it right away. You'll have some to apply for bathing, washing your clothes, and ingesting. Just maintain in thoughts to purify it first before consuming.

2.Wells

Wells are incredible sources of water for the motive that they will be sustainable. Know your vicinity and find out if there may be a well nearby that you may get water from.

3.Rivers and streams

Not all water coming from herbal assets like streams and rivers is secure to drink. One sip from one wrong supply, and also you'll come to be floating downstream. There are large chances that your streams and rivers were polluted with poisonous waste. Serious ailments can broaden from eating unpurified water, and natural bodies of water are wealthy with micro organism, chemical run-off, parasites, and distinctive waste merchandise that could be fatal for you. There is not any exception to the guideline of thumb of purifying your water first earlier than eating it.

4.Salt and brackish water

Salt and brackish water are higher left by myself. You might probable want immoderate purification earlier than they can be used for ingesting. However, you could constantly use them for unique household purposes like cleaning and flushing the rest room.

Chapter 8: Clean Water

Having water, extra especially, having secure water, is a basic need. In our preoccupation with imparting ourselves with the necessities to stay on, it will likely be easy to miss subjects which incorporates meals and water safety. Save your self from experiencing unnecessary and bulky ailments while you're in the midst of a disaster and inventory up on steady and purified water.

1.Boiling

If you don't have any water purification system accessible, you can continually bypass again to the fundamentals and boil your water for at least five mins to kill the dangerous pathogens that would make your water dangerous for ingesting.

2.Microfilters

Microfilters can be used to treat water as they are able to disposing of bacteria from it. As micro organism and protozoans are the maximum commonplace organisms that may be determined in a single's eating water, it's miles a need to to eliminate them. Microfilters with pore sizes of no massive than 0.Three microns are required for a hit filtration. Glass fibers, plastics, and ceramics can be used as filtration media.

3.Chemical disinfectants

Chlorine, for one, can be used as an agent to deal with water. Its effect is short and it's without issues available to everybody. But like distinctive chemical disinfectants, chlorine doesn't hold any lengthy-term effect. After a while, water will become infected over again because of extended garage. This isn't useful for consuming capabilities.

4.Conventional family bleach

Bleach that is used inside the family can also be done to purify water. For one gallon of water, you can add 16 drops of ordinary family unscented liquid bleach to sanitize it.

But, you may handiest use this for cleansing capabilities, this is not beneficial for consuming.

Chapter 9: Water Storage

The water deliver can be close to off with none statement of at the same time because it's going to head again. Especially at some point of herbal disasters, you may want to rely on your private water assets to keep away from dehydration and carry out primary own family sports activities.

As for the amount of water that you have to keep, it's far encouraged to preserve a gallon of water for each person in line with day for at least three days or how many days you are afraid the water supply gained't be back on. There want to moreover be sufficient reserved water for circle of relatives capabilities at the side of cleaning, bathing, and cooking. You ought to take into consideration your norms and necessities. If you think a gallon of water in line with day for one person obtained't be enough due to the truth he makes use of a number of water often, you should keep more.

Do not be afraid to have an excessive amount of water. The extra you've got, the better.

Now, your next assignment need to be on in which to store your water. Bottles are the most apparent preference for water storage. However, buying in bulk can be high priced, so that you have the choice to store your water on an to be had field that you have. But it might be first-rate in case you remembered to take on the important precautions to keep the cleanliness of your water and your difficulty.

Here are some topics to maintain in mind whilst storing water:

1.Use bins which can be meals-grade in storing water.

When you operate other types of boxes other than that of meals-grade in managing water, you run the danger of dangerous materials and chemical substances leaking into your water. In addition, do now not located your water in metal containers due to the fact the metallic will corrode. Opt for glass, plastic, or stainless steel as an opportunity.

2.Do not use bins that have been formerly used for some exclusive type of beverage.

Avoid using packing containers which have formerly contained milk or juice, for example. With plastic bottles, specifically, materials from the previous beverage will maintain on with the plastic regardless of how an awful lot you easy it. Your juice, for one, consists of sugar as a way to purpose bacteria growth, so don't located your water into its box.

3.Remember to clean your bins.

Before storing your water inside the bins, make sure that they have got been sanitized nicely. Wash them with heat water and cleaning cleaning soap and rinse thoroughly before filling them with water, and don't forget about to hold your arms far from the pinnacle of the bottle at the same time as you're filling it up.

4.Rotate and check your water frequently.

It is right to frequently take a look at your stored water to ensure that it's though potable. Even despite the fact that you've met each important measure to make it actually drinkable, there are some of techniques in which your water can become infected. If you need to smooth the containers, losing water might be a horrible idea. Instead of dumping it, you could use the water for outstanding family chores like cleaning and laundry. You can also purify the water again to make it stable for cooking and eating.

Chapter 10: Common Mistakes When

Building A Shelter

Here are the not unusual errors that people make even as building their very very own safe haven:

1.Too large and open

When it comes to region, human beings commonly make their secure haven huge and open. There are not any issues together together with your safe haven's duration so long as you don't make it open sufficient for a hyena or a mugger to are available. You want to make sure that your door isn't always massive open to protect your self from an invasion of unwanted factors.

2.An twist of fate within the making

Perhaps because of inexperience and wrong facts, human beings make the error of building shelters that may disintegrate on their population. Before you try to create one, you want to educate your self first on what's required to construct a strong one. Make certain which you recognise the manner to set up the structural basis as it guarantees balance.

three.Overestimating warm temperature

You have been useless tired as you were building your stable haven, so you were given sloppy. That isn't always any excuse. Or likely you were injured, and you couldn't do any higher. That is suitable, however the fact despite the fact that remains that you'll probable turn to a human Popsicle.

If you notion that setting one flimsy blanket at the floor to hold you heat is sufficient to protect you from the cold of the night, then you definately're — truely — useless wrong. In constructing your non-public safe haven, one of the utmost priorities is insulation. Don't just suppose that because of the reality your secure haven appears actual, it's miles going to enjoy great. Before you fall asleep, make sure that your safe haven is snow fall and typhoon-evidence. In case it will become too hot for you, you could open it a hint bit to allow in some air.

4.Wrong preference of elevation

A mistake that people frequently devote is constructing their shelters on clearly high grounds. Higher elevations will now not preserve you hotter as they may display you to the wind. Moreover, hearth is extra hard to assemble and preserve because of the fact the warm temperature may be carried away from you with the useful resource of the wind, and fuel is probably burned quicker. Drier areas covered from the elements on decrease grounds will constantly be your outstanding desire.

How to Build a Basic Shelter?

The shelter is one of the simple dreams because it gives critical factors for someone's survival. It affords safety to someone and moreover an avenue to keep one warm temperature. In unlucky situations in which you want to waft from your home or have out of vicinity one, you could create or purchase various types of essential shelters to your community keep.

1.Tents

Tents aren't supposed to be permanent shelters but can be used as short strategies of retaining some distance from volatile factors. To an amount, it gives some protection in competition to animals and could hold you heat. Preppers normally pick out tents whilst looking ahead to short-time period emergencies and encompass commercially produced tents in their survival kits.

It might be exceptional in case you and your own family recognize beforehand to put up a tent. You can spend a weekend far from home, like tenting, to learn how to live in a tent with none get proper of entry to to modern era and luxuries. This form of interest will assist increase your survival abilties and helps you to have right mindset.

2.Caves

If you recognize your terrain ahead, you can search for caves wherein you may live in brief. Remember to test the region for any insects or wild animals that would pose a hazard to you before you inhabit any place.

three.Using materials within the wild

Especially in instances on the identical time as you turn out to be within the wild, you may employ what nature can offer. Tree limbs, leaves, and rocks may be implemented to end up structures of a make-shift safe haven.

Part five

Other Important Things

Chapter 11: Building Your Own Fire

It is maximum in all likelihood that you may

lose electricity, particularly in post-catastrophe situations. Electrical strains can be down, and your electric powered powered stove is pretty loads useless in this case. Moreover, permit us to no longer neglect the fact which you could probably come to be in the wild or with out a domestic, so domestic device could not be internal your acquire despite the truth that they'll be running.

One of the maximum essential skills which you have to analyze in schooling for failures is fireside-constructing. Fire is a person's high-quality friend. Unless you could stomach sushi and uncooked meat for each meal of every day and one way or the alternative have the refrigeration for that, you need hearth to prepare dinner dinner and boil your water. Most importantly, you want it to hold you heat and alive.

Moreover, it might furthermore provide illumination for you and a way to beat back animals.

Since you can in no manner tell what form of catastrophe may moreover strike, you need to educate your self on the one of a type techniques of constructing your personal hearth to have a reservoir of capabilities to expose off while the state of affairs arises. And thoughts you, each different ideal trouble approximately getting ready for this assignment is that you do not need to pressure yourself out through rubbing two stones together to create a spark. Now, you can equip yourself with the essential gadget to help you collect a fireplace without troubles.

1.Matches

Using fits is the vintage-age approach of beginning a fire, in order that they want to be part of your survival bundle. Avail of water-evidence fits if you could discover any or positioned the normal ones in water resistant bins to ensure that you could have a walking fireside in anything climate you will be experiencing. It may additionally be higher to pick out wooden fits over paper ones.

2.Firesticks

There are pretty a few firesticks supplied at camping stores. Firesticks are as an alternative clean to keep because of the truth that they may be small, and there are types which you use even in case your kindling is damp.

three.Lighters

It will also be available to maintain a couple of lighters with you. They are very easy to apply and may be reused, not like suits. Butane ones are tremendous for windy and moist conditions, genuinely so they'll be most famous. You want to make sure which you deliver extra refills to your lighters.

4.Ferrocerium

Ferrocerium produces intensely hot sparks whilst scraped in competition to distinct metals and specific textured surfaces. Ferrocerium rods are high-quality additions to your fireplace-beginning package in advance than they may paintings in wet or dry environments. They also are available transportable sizes.

Chapter 12: Maintaining Proper Hygiene

It might be so clean to overlook sanitation and proper hygiene in a time even as your every idea is zeroed in on surviving. But it's far an hassle that you want to no longer forget because of the truth illnesses and illnesses want to boom from incorrect hygiene.

I preference that thru now, you apprehend that contact with fecal be counted (poo) – can be negative for your health. Dysentery, diarrhea, cholera, and plenty of others., are simply a number of the feasible illnesses you can collect with out proper sanitation.

Since water may be an trouble and also you don't want to waste it on flushing the bathroom, human waste can also need to be set free someplace else.

1.Composting lavatories

Composting lavatories are to be had at on-line or community tenting shops. They are perfect for the proper and clean disposal of wasters. Some fashions separate beverages from solids, and your waste ultimately finally ends up in a sealed bucket and could be handled with bleach to eliminate micro organism and different disorder-causing parasites. This way, you could optimistically sell off your waste into your latrine without any fear of contamination—one thing which you want to don't forget - in no way cast off your waste close to a water deliver.

2.Buckets

Disaster time isn't any fancy time. So, in case you do now not have a few other opportunity or if composting toilets are too high priced in your price range, you can constantly pick out a bucket blanketed with a garbage bag.

You may need a large bucket, in all likelihood a 5-gallon one, thick rubbish baggage, and lime. Line your bucket with the heavy-obligation garbage bag, and after doing all of your commercial enterprise

enterprise, cover it with chlorinated lime and location the lid of the bucket decrease returned on. Once the rubbish bag begins to get filled, seal it up, take it out of the bucket, and replace it with a contemporary one.

three.Latrines

Dig a latrine nearby to manipulate your waste. But yet again, maintain in mind not to try this near a potential water deliver. If there may be a frame of water close by, dig your latrine as a minimum hundred feet far from it. For a latrine that a couple of humans can appoint, dig one this is as a minimum one and a half of of toes good sized and 1 foot deep. Stock up on chlorinated lime so that you can cover your waste with it whenever you defecate. Other alternatives to lime can be timber ash or kitty litter. Additionally, count on times approximately digging a latrine if you stay in a place prone to flooding, as making one could probably not be a realistic preference.

4.Cat holes

Cat holes sound lovely, proper? They moreover appearance adorable and are one of the best and fastest techniques to keep hygiene rapid. Dig a small hollow of approximately eight inches deep and faraway from a water supply and do your company. Do no longer neglect about to cowl the hollow up whilst you are completed.

Aside from proper methods of waste disposal, there are greater stuff you want to preserve in thoughts regarding the issue of hygiene.

Add on your stockpile listing severa rest room paper. Secure a roll of bathroom paper for one man or woman consistent with week and modify it relying on the need. Males and women can also range in the quantity they need, so remember whilst you are stocking up. In addition, you have were given you acquire rubbish bags for definitely every person for their person sanitation needs.

Chlorinated lime or one of a kind alternatives is also a ought to in your kit and for girls, don't forget to inventory up on woman hygiene products like sanitary napkins and tampons.

If viable, use biodegradable bags as a good buy as you may and ensure that they won't effects break down on the equal time as included up in your bucket.

Chapter 13: Learn First Aid

First useful useful resource can be very

crucial. You actually can't get wounded and expect to have it healed after licking it or looking in advance to the natural restoration way to paintings. In conditions like those, you need to be on top of your undertaking and searching ahead to a wound — mainly a debilitating one — to heal with out treating it would be incredibly disadvantageous to you.

Aside from storing up at the vital additives of your first beneficial useful resource package, you furthermore also can need to both have an tremendous guide indicating the makes use of and alertness of each item in your package deal or, ideally, study them firsthand. Listed beneath are the subjects that need to be present in your first-useful resource package that will help you beat the percentages for the duration of calamities. There are pre-stocked first-aid kits to be had from stores, so you can purchase them and upload your drug treatments and one-of-a-kind more factors for wound management into the kit.

1. Latex or sterile gloves

2. Antibiotic ointment

3. Adhesive bandages in simply one in every of a kind sizes

4. Sterile dressings for bleedings

five. Thermometer

6. Soap and exquisite cleansing marketers

7. Face Towels

8.Burn ointment

9.Decontaminants

10. Prescription medications of contributors you are prepping for (e.G., bronchial hypersensitive reactions inhalers, insulin, anti-hypersensitivity)

eleven. Anti-diarrhea medication

12. Pain relievers

thirteen. Laxatives

14. Antacids

15. Lubricant

16. Scissors

17. Tweezers

If you show as a whole lot as be available within the wild, keep in mind that medicinal plant life can help address a wound. But, you ought to make yourself familiar with their specific makes use of. For instance, blackberries can do plenty to your belly apart from genuinely satiating it. Blackberry leaves are beneficial in treating diarrhea. And in case you want to repel bugs and worm bites, procure a few lavender or neem leaves. Always exercise the critical care even as you're the usage of flowers from the wild. If you are not 100% positive about the purpose of a selected plant, do not chance it. The same goes for ingesting these flowers.

One of the myths approximately outdoor survival that can be pretty deadly is the claim that you can eat and use the whole thing within the wild. With proper information, you can recognize that there are poisonous vegetation and mushrooms available a very good way to ease your struggling, first-class because of the truth they will deliver you to the afterlife, that is form of what we're looking for to avoid right here.

Chapter 14: Preparing A Bug-Out Bag

In the absence of the luxuries we can be used to within the current-day worldwide, you want to make do with what is to be had in instances of disaster.

Every prepper need to have a Bug-Out Bag prepared. A Bug-Out Bag or BOB is one which includes your kits and severa gadgets to help you stay on within the face of herbal calamities, wars, and other lifestyles-threatening screw ups. It may be personalized to be suitable for a specific period.

BOB's are designed to be transportable so you can take them with you inside the event which you need to go away your house in a direct. There is not any consistent gadget for the right BOB as it might depend upon your area and the capability threats you may be coping with.

A lot of situations ought to name for which you leave your house. From natural catastrophes to social uprisings, the ones activities can come unexpectedly. So, it might help if you were in your ft and be organized for some thing. Besides being well-informed and professional in incredible survival abilties, you furthermore mght want to very own a hard and fast of resources and machine to resource your survival. And maintaining these tools in a single bag is an effective manner to get the hell out of an emergency in a unmarried piece. You received't need to run throughout the house seeking out what you have due to the fact the whole thing is already in a single area.

I surely have listed below the stuff you need to preserve in mind in getting equipped your BOB.

1.Purpose

In getting ready your BOB, you need to have a smooth motive in thoughts. What is your BOB for? Will you operate it for a long time, or is it simply transferring from one region to a few different? This element is an important step in getting your BOB ready as it will can help you realise how a first-rate deal or how little of an item you need to deliver.

2.Travel records

The distance and the terrain you'll be traveling in are essential elements to pay attention to. When you try to flow into far from human beings from extremely good international locations taking pictures the hell out of every first rate or, permit us to say, on foot far from an incoming tsunami (God bless you), speed is extensive. Your BOB shouldn't be so heavy that you may't take a few steps beforehand. The heavier it's miles, the slower you may run some distance from trouble. You additionally need to upload into the equation your bodily capabilities. As someone who no longer frequently does any form of physical interest, a 40-pound of BOB will probably be the lack of life of you.

If you're touring prolonged distances, you could motive for BOBs weighing a complete of twelve kilos. If you want to move amongst elements A and B, a twenty-pound BOB will do.

This is wherein trial runs might be most beneficial for. Take out your BOBs for trial runs and see if you are snug with its weight. Be sincere concerning what your frame can take, and don't push it.

3.Shelter and warmth

Always make certain that your BOB includes your device for constructing a safe haven. Shelter training is particularly critical because finishing up frozen to dying due to inadequate safety is exactly what you're attempting not to do. Fact is, you may stay on three weeks without meals and 3 days with out water, but a night time with hypothermia will kill you without delay. Hone your competencies in building a shelter, buy strong and robust objects, and don't pass reasonably-priced in this element because of the reality at the same time as you are building a faulty tent, a undergo might be on its manner to devour you.

4.Hydration

Carrying bottles packed with water is a splendid concept, but it may be difficult to convey a % heavy with water. So, what you need to solid in your BOB are your water purification equipment to clean out any water you could find out in any our bodies of water close by. However, you need to find out first if there are belongings of water in which you are heading due to the reality otherwise, your equipment will become vain; if so, you will need to deliver bottles of water to remain hydrated.

5.Food

The query is that this: how lengthy do you be aware your self to be had? Answer that query and make it a base for a way a good deal food you need to hold with you. To preserve region and weight, human beings typically encompass power bars and canned food in their BOBs. But this doesn't advocate that they will be the great matters which you'll be eating. They are imagined to provide you energy and sustenance at the start, enough that you could engage in different techniques of obtaining meals which include looking, fishing, foraging, and trapping. But take be conscious that the ones strategies can first-rate be completed with the ideal earlier knowledge and competencies. Your tools, I reiterate, can be vain if you do now not apprehend the manner to use them.

Additionally, even as setting MREs and freeze-dried meals in your BOB, be aware of the quantity of place and weight that you can manipulate to pay for to lose for your canned and heavy goods.

6.Hygiene and First Aid

Have an sufficient supply of the drugs which you want. Prepare what you need for your hypersensitive reactions because of the truth finding a drug hold can be a undertaking at the equal time as you're handy seeking out to survive. Make positive as well that your first beneficial useful resource package is properly-prepared. Don't without a doubt take delivery of a package whole of Band-Aids because of the truth that might rarely assist whilst you're bleeding or poisoned or stabbed to loss of life. Even the smallest of cuts can turn without a doubt complicated because of infections, so you need to invest in proper treatment.

Stock up your BOBs together together with your hygiene package deal. This includes shampoo, soap, toothbrush, washcloth, menstrual hygiene products, deodorant, relaxation room papers, and so forth.

7.Fire Starting

If you've been pushed into the outdoors because of wars or herbal screw ups, you are as properly as useless without fireplace and warmth for a sizeable length. It is probably amazing if you placed out to start a fire under any weather situation. Prepare your fits, tinder, fireside sticks, lighters, or some thing else in an effort to help build a fire.

eight.Light

Preparing lighting, mainly transportable ones, is a must due to the fact it is most in all likelihood that power can be reduce off in the course of failures, and it might be hard to recognize a element in the front of you at night time time even as there's no illumination. A sun-charged light that doesn't want any battery might be quality, further to candles. You can also solid camp lighting fixtures or headlamps. Invest in excellent lights to now not have any regrets whilst night time comes.

nine.Clothing

Clothing isn't non-obligatory and is really an item which you want to characteristic on your BOB. You want to prepare greater devices of garments and ensure that they're suitable for the climate. For chillier climates, jackets and prolonged pants are critical. And in no state of affairs need to you placed on shorts irrespective of the climate. Even at the identical time as it's miles heat available, your legs want safety from the warm temperature of the sun. Not to mention that wearing prolonged pants will decrease your pores and skin's possibilities of having irritated with allergens and getting bitten by way of the usage of bugs.

In addition, keep your ft from injuries by way of carrying an splendid set of footwear. Change your socks as regularly as feasible and wash them properly. If there's enough area for your p.C., prepare devices of shoes that you could alternate relying on the scenario and region. Choose footwear which you're cushty taking walks in. There's no time to think about what's fashionable as you get away from toppling wood or risky u . S . Invaders.

10. Bug-Out Bags

Don't be too frugal with reference to your BOB, and in no way accept a reasonably-priced backpack with horrible fine. Trust me, they will tear aside, and also you'll grow to be collectively together with your subjects at the ground.

You want to invest in a notable backpack because it's far in which your gear for survival are contained. Resort to heavier packs due to the fact they'll be inclined to be thicker and further durable in assessment to extremely-mild ones. And don't forget: take out your BOBS for trial runs with a motive to test its effectiveness. These trial runs will will let you apprehend of capability problems with the gadgets you've got were given prepared.

Part 6

Financial Prepping

Chapter 15: Is Your Money Ready?

Much has been said about getting geared up for doomsday because of wars or herbal

screw ups. Books were written about tactics to find property of water and stockpiling meals as a way to live on the entire period of the calamities. However, what humans fail to famend is some different form of event that could disrupt the food deliver and trigger social unrest – an economic disaster.

It's now not out of the query that an monetary instability massive sufficient to cause regular living dysfunctions need to occur. Financial markets are quite volatile and touchy, at the same time as stock markets are with out trouble affected by politics and social events. The growing charge of oil, which may be attributed to political unrest, may want to cause corresponding increases in fees of every day items and impact people's capacity to live truly at their technique.

In reality, some of personal and small-scale monetary catastrophes get up each day. Institutions near due to economic disaster, houses foreclosed, and people lose their jobs due to the truth corporations are in massive debt. In times like the ones, human beings are left without an earnings to maintain the desires of their households. Imagine what could probably manifest if a global financial disaster takes place.

Financial prepping is simply as critical as making it a trouble that you have sufficient substances to ultimate you sooner or later of the rainy days due to the fact, like herbal calamities, economic turmoil could also rob you of the chance to live on.

Therefore, it is important that you moreover devise a method, so you received't get blind-sided in case of vital economic disasters.

1.Simplify budget

Stop spending on vain and indulgent subjects. When you have already got a sensible one, a present day vacuum cleanser will now not do you any accurate if you have nothing to devour. As heaps as possible, discover ways to live a minimalist but sensible lifestyles. Think several times in advance than you purchase any product and ask yourself in case you really need that object. Ultimately, the purpose is to lessen your expenditure and boom your financial savings so you can find the money for to acquire fundamental necessities in some unspecified time in the destiny of hard instances.

2.Eliminate any kind of debt, mainly the adjustable ones

Debts will chunk you in the ass most on the same time as you don't want it to. Credit gambling cards, as an instance, exist in an environment that depends on inflation. When a monetary disaster hits, banks might be forced to raise charges to make up their losses, and also you'd want to shoulder that increase.

three.Invest in what should make you self-enough

Spend coins best on necessities. As meals can come to be scarce or inaccessible sooner or later of some thing type of disaster, it is probably a fantastic go along with the flow to invest in them in addition to in water and gasoline. You can choose to allot a few cash on growing vegetation and fruit timber to have a steady meals supply to install your desk. Additionally, you should purchase critical devices so you can come up with shopping for strength if it ever comes to a degree on the same time as the financial device devolves right into a bartering tool. Case in point, storing a bag of sugar can likely assure you a month's nicely really worth of hire.

4.Save

Saving is one of the most critical steps in prepping for a economic catastrophe. When saving, you essentially choose amongst excessive frugality while the demand arises and slow/moderate frugality. You can be forced to significantly limit your budget and modify whilst a disaster hits due to the reality you'd be obliged to. Now, this will be exceedingly difficult due to the truth you're exposing yourself to a exercise which you haven't tried in advance than in any other case you don't have a statistics in. Imagine that from $4 in line with meal, you are pushed to reduce it to $2 due to monetary constraints. Not only ought to this situation be hard to belly before the whole lot, however it might additionally take a toll for your nicely-being. The better opportunity can be to encompass moderate frugality step by step. As early as nowadays, analyze and try and stay inner your manner. Try to evaluate what you can stay without and collect yourself a financial cushion via way of spending most effective what is critical and cushty sufficient.

Don't wonder your self into doing drastic measures like doing without belongings which is probably formerly available to you. Let's say which you were used to food that charge a hundred dollars. Don't straight away soar into decreasing it to 20-five in a unmarried blink. Make yourself snug with a lesser and lesser budget for food in each meal until you locate the proper stability amongst delight and frugality. Start constructing an emergency fund.

Saving doesn't moreover suggest which you are required to surrender everything which you have these days. Learn to understand what is essential and prioritize practicality over extravagance.

1.Budget

Budget and maintain music of your income and charges. Those which can be non-crucial to every day residing want to be cut out of your charge variety. Proper allocation to excellent important gadgets in conjunction with food, utilities, transportation, financial savings, amongst others, need to be determined.

2.Sell non-important gadgets

For extra earnings, you could also get rid of devices which you not use. Make an stock of factors which might be redundant or can also want to most effective upload greater rate even as applied. You can placed them up inside the path of a garage sale or sell them on eBay.

3.Learn DIY skills

DIY talents will no longer great are to be had in handy for survival, however they also can lessen you plenty of expenses in case you learn how to do subjects which you may first of all pay for. Learning them may additionally advocate that you prevent paying exorbitant prices to different human beings for executing obligations that you could very well preserve near to your personal. Some of the considered necessary abilities that a prepper want to understand encompass first aid, automobile and bicycle protection, appliance repair, meals protection, water treatment, self-safety, looking and fishing, home maintenance, out of doors survival, guns training, and so on.

Now, the following query is in which to have a look at those abilties. There are numerous options open for you. You can normally sign up for your network college or avail yourself of community assets. There are numerous communities that provide free courses on emergency preparedness.

The Internet is some distinctive real desire as it is a hub of information. Videos and unique manuals on various topics are to be had online so one can have a observe, and the variety of talents you may hone thru the Internet is endless.

If you're a extra traditional form of learner, you can usually visit the library and borrow books at the subjects you're inquisitive about.

Chapter 16: Survival First Aid

Before going into the nitty-gritty of disaster survival, you want to examine the basics of first resource. Odds are, you or a member of the family will get harm inside the course of the primary few moments of a disaster, and due to that you want to learn how to treat easy accidents in advance than they turn out to be a real trouble later. In this financial ruin, you could learn how to maximize the use of the primary useful useful resource kits that you can typically buy in outdoor hobby shops, and what you may do if you one manner or the alternative run out of substances and have to hotel to Mother Nature to provide for you.

Cleaning and dressing wounds

On regular days, small cuts and scrapes are not that huge of a deal; you without a doubt spray some antiseptic on the wound after which slap a band useful resource on it and you're proper to move. However, in a survival state of affairs, subjects aren't that easy. For one hassle, you could most likely be outdoor and underneath the mercy of the environment, which means that there's a plethora of germs and bacteria obtainable that's definitely itching to get into your wounds and purpose excessive infections. This is why you want to smooth and dress your wounds proper now; it does no longer undergo in thoughts if it's far most effective a small reduce or scratch.

The first detail which you need to do is find out genuinely how extreme the wound in fact is. If there's bleeding, it's far quality to stem the blood drift in advance than you without a doubt start cleaning the wound. One manner to sluggish down the bleeding, and in all likelihood even forestall it, is to elevate the wounded body difficulty above the coronary coronary heart degree. If this isn't viable, comply with a moderate quantity of strain over the wound to forestall the blood go with the flow.

Once you've got were given stopped the bleeding, you can then proceed to clean and disinfect the wound. However, earlier than you study any medication, you want to rinse the wound the use of lukewarm water to easy away any dirt or dust that might have found their manner into the wound. All first useful useful resource kits encompass a beneficiant quantity of antiseptics, normally in spray bottles for smooth software.

A key component to don't forget whilst utilising antiseptics is to artwork from the inner of the wound and head in the direction of the outside. This is crucial because you need don't want to pull any dirt into the wound; you want to easy the wound as plenty as feasible earlier than you take a look at a bandage. Start by way of the usage of wiping small circles and artwork your way out of doors of the wound. You should moreover easy the outside of the wound as well; you want to smooth a place this is more or much less two times the dimensions of the actual wound itself.

After cleaning the wound, you may practice a topical antibiotic at the wound. This medicinal drug absolutely serves features: the primary issue is that the medicine will assist the wound heal quicker, and second, the ointment will prevent the bandage from sticking onto the wound, making it less difficult to update the dressing every time favored.

On the problem of bandages, it's far brilliant to use large strips in choice to the tiny band-aids which you use for paper cuts and minor injuries. 2 x 2 bandages are high-quality because they offer enough coverage for maximum wounds and you could constantly stack or extra of them for massive accidents. Don't skimp on bandages, you want to make certain which you cover up the wound actually to save you infections and contaminations. In case you find yourself in a situation in which it's miles in all likelihood that your wounds may additionally get wet, you need to wrap gauze bandage liberally over the wounded place.

It is usually recommended which you update the dressing every day, and whilst you do you want to easy the wound all once more. Do this often until the wound has completely healed.

Making a makeshift splint and sling for broken limbs

Besides cuts and scrapes, it is also very likely that you'll be bothered by way of sprained joints and maybe even a broken bone or . The way to ensure that those types of injuries do now not get any worse is by means of using way of immobilizing the injured body detail the usage of a splint or a sling.

Before you learn how to make splints and slings, you want to examine a bit about fractures. There are two kinds of fractures;

the open fractures wherein the bone breaks through the pores and skin, and closed fractures wherein there may be no open wound, however there would possibly in all likelihood although be damaged blood vessels below the skin. An damage is a closed fracture the affected place should be a piece numb, is cool to the touch, and if the man or woman is in surprise. If the very last symptom is gift, there might be a severed essential blood vessel and the individual is tormented by large inner bleeding.

Now that you have a few concept on the way to discover fractures, you may start analyzing a manner to make a makeshift splint. The remarkable factor about splints is you could cause them to the use of any moderate and stiff cloth that you may discover. In most cases, you can make a splint using a dry, strong tree branch. To make a primary splint, take , appreciably straight away tree branches, wrap a piece of padding fabric round them (like a few cloth), vicinity the sticks on contrary aspects of the injured region, and then the use of any shape of cordage, lash the sticks securely throughout the affected body aspect. Be cautious not to tie the cordage too tightly otherwise you danger slicing off blood circulate.

Making a sling is a piece less complicated, you clearly need portions of material, one this is huge enough to wrap throughout the affected individual (spherical forty" x 40"), and an prolonged skinny strip. Fold the huge piece of cloth diagonally, forming a triangle, and then drape it over the chest of the affected individual. One corner of the triangle must be dangling over the unharmed shoulder, and the lowest corner need to maintain just underneath the waist. Lift this backside nook up truly enough to manual the weight of the injured arm, ensure that the hand is barely protruding out of doors the edge of the material. Tie the corner draped over the unharmed shoulder with the lowest corner you lifted up, certainly inside the lower back of the neck. To make certain that the injured detail is absolutely immobilized, wrap the lengthy piece of cloth across the frame of the affected man or woman; ensure that it's miles placed above the injured place and under the unhurt arm.

Cardio-pulmonary resuscitation (CPR)

One of the maximum important first beneficial resource abilties which you need to investigate, know-how CPR may additionally definitely permit you to maintain someone else's existence.

Begin chest compressions

Before you even start doing some detail, you ought to first take a look at if the individual stays breathing. If the person stopped breathing, place the bottom of your hand inside the middle of the chest after which region your other end it. Push down over the chest the usage of your body weight; the chest of the sufferer want to move down via as a minimum inches. You also can experience some disconcerting snaps and pops in the course of the primary few pumps, but don't fear as this is absolutely ordinary. Make positive that the individual's chest recoiled truely in advance than doing every other compression. Do this constantly at a fee of a hundred pumps a minute as a minimum.

Begin rescue respiratory

After round thirty compressions, if the sufferer continues to be now not respiration, you may want to begin rescue respiratory. First, you want to open the victim's airway by using the use of lifting the pinnacle up multiple inches off the ground. Pinch the nostrils to prevent air from escaping and vicinity your mouth over the sufferer's; make certain which you make a entire seal at some stage in the mouth. Blow into the victim's mouth; your breaths must be strong sufficient to make the sufferer's chest upward thrust. Once the victim's chest goes down, deliver them every other breath. If you find out that the victim's chest isn't developing irrespective of how hard you blow, the airway should now not be easy. Reposition the victim's head through raising it a chunk greater and attempt once more.

Keep doing chest compressions and rescue respiration till you observe that the sufferer can begin respiratory on his or her private. The cycle must be 30 chest compressions then 2 rescue breaths and then begin with the chest compressions again.

Medicinal Plants

You fine have a restricted quantity of drug remedies on your prepper First Aid package deal, and you need to make them final for as long as feasible. However, if you do run out of scientific assets, you have to now not be concerned because of the reality Mother

Nature has a whole apothecary of natural drugs that you may use.

Aloe Vera – This is one of the most versatile medicinal plant life because it literally has dozens of uses. However, maximum humans use Aloe Vera to deal with and disinfect minor cuts and burns. To use Aloe Vera, clearly choose a leaf, scrape off the thorns, wreck it in half of of, after which rub the uncovered gel onto the affected location.

Garlic – Besides giving your pasta a miles wanted flavor burst, garlic really has more than one medicinal makes use of as well. Garlic has sturdy antibiotic homes so that you can use it to deal with moderate infections. One of the super techniques to make use of the medicinal consequences of garlic is through making an oil infusion. Just chop a whole bunch of garlic cloves, enough to fill a small mason jar, and then pour sufficient olive oil to cover the chopped garlic. Let the oil steep for regular with week in advance than straining it thru cheesecloth and into an amber colored jar.

Valerian — Many people use this herb to cope with exquisite ailments, particularly insomnia and tension. To use Valerian, you need to pick out a gaggle of the leaves and make tea out of them. The amusing homes of Valerian will help calm your thoughts and beautify your cognizance, which you could really need masses of inside the course of a survival scenario.

Echinacea — This flowering plant has numerous medicinal uses. When floor into a paste, you could use it to make minor cuts and scrapes heal faster way to its antibacterial houses. You also can make an immune tool boosting tea out of the flowers and leaves; that is pretty handy at the equal time because the SHTF and also you don't have easy get right of get entry to to to medical services.

Lemon Balm — Many of the maximum deadly ailments come from mosquito bites, so you should do everything you could to prevent them from attaching themselves to every little little bit of uncovered pores and pores and skin. If you don't have any bug repellent to your First Aid Kit, you ought to look for some wild lemon balm. All you want to do is overwhelm a handful of the leaves and exercising the extremely good-smelling paste for your pores and pores and skin. Apparently, mosquitoes and unique biting bugs aren't keen on the heady scent of lemon balm.

Sage — Not quality is that this kitchen staple terrific at such as taste to fish and chicken dishes, it also has severa useful clinical makes use of. For instance, you can make a tea out of the leaves to help address indigestion. In addition, if you occur to run out of gauze pads, the gentle sage leaves can without a doubt make a very good alternative.

Feverfew – Many humans preserve in mind this flowering plant a weed, and they might pull it out of their lawns on the mere sight of it. However, Feverfew tea is in truth an extraordinary pain reliever, and as its call indicates, it may assist decrease fevers.

Lavender – This flowering plant not best lets in humans lighten up, it additionally has super antiseptic homes. Crush a handful of plant life and leaves and observe the ensuing paste at the wounds to save you infections. You can also use lavender as a ache reliever; this is particularly effective for treating sunburns and painful rashes.

As you may see, you don't must panic if you phrase that your First Aid elements are dwindling. You can find out an entire lot of worthwhile replacements in nature; you absolutely need to recognize what to search for and what they may be able to do.

Chapter 17: Basics Of Prepping

Survival coaching, or prepping because the advocates name it, is the approach of creating prepared your circle of relatives for any untoward incident that can appear in the near destiny. Prepping includes storing sufficient food and water to make sure survival for at least every week or so in case deliver chains are reduce off. You need to additionally keep in mind teaching anybody within the family on the way to continue to exist in case some difficulty forces you out of the residence and into the wild, and exceptional capabilities that could are available beneficial if ever the worst-case state of affairs does take region.

You can't inform what form of herbal or guy-made catastrophe will strike and even as it's going to show up, so it is superb to take a look at all the fundamentals of prepping certainly so you can cowl all of your bases.

Water

Humans can live on for 3 mins with out air, 3 days without water, and three weeks with out meals. Since only some times will motive a scarcity of breathable air, and those times aren't often survivable, you need to first attention on storing sufficient water for you and your family's survival.

The rule of thumb for water garage is to typically have a gallon of water in line with individual, in case you need to live on for seventy two hours after a primary disaster (this is the general rule). You need to have at the least 3 gallons of water stowed away carefully in your house; multiply that quantity with the resource of the variety of humans to your own family.

Now which you have a hard estimate of just how a lot water you can want for emergencies, the following difficulty that you want to recall is in which to hold them. Unlike food, water takes a number of storage space because of the reality it's far incompressible. The only factor that you could do to hold area is to hold your water in 5-gallon plastic jugs. This manner, you could keep greater water in a restrained area in evaluation to storing instances of individual water bottles.

Besides storing water, you need to additionally have a few water treatment capsules to your prepper stores. In case your water deliver runs out, but there's a herbal water supply close by, you could use water remedy drugs to disinfect the water and make it potable. On the opportunity hand, if you do no longer have water remedy pills, you can use a capful of laundry bleach to deal with up to a few gallons of water.

Food

The one element that you need to hold in mind at the same time as storing meals for emergencies is that the majority of them, if not all, need to be non-perishable. This approach you can store them with out the want for refrigeration, this is crucial due to the fact the number one trouble to move at some stage in and after a top disaster is the strength deliver. If all of your meals is within the freezer and the power goes out, you extraordinary have a couple of hours in advance than all of your substances begin to pass horrible.

The most obvious meals substances you have to stock up on are canned goods. Canning successfully offers months or years to the shelf life of maximum food. You can get precise kinds of foods like sausages, sardines, tuna, veggies, and others.

On the alternative hand, in case you are planning to store your meals longer, you need to get freeze-dried food. You can pick out from a huge style of freeze-dried food from extremely good manufacturer's in recent times (high quality, there are numerous corporations which may be catering to the desires of preppers). These meals can preserve for as a minimum 10 to twenty years and you really want to characteristic water to cause them to palatable. Don't fear; freeze-dried meals these days aren't as bland as they emerge as as soon as, in truth, an entire lot of them without a doubt taste quite suitable.

If you have got were given a huge sufficient plot of land in your house, you could moreover try your hand on gardening and small animal husbandry. These strategies do require a piece of talent, but once you get the draw close of them you can sincerely have a self-retaining gadget. This is excellent for while the aftermath of the catastrophe takes a whole lot longer as predicted to lower, this is a likely opportunity if you consider it.

Chapter 18: Bushcraft Basics

"If you adore books. You will love the Lean Stone Book Club"

To discover extra, truly click on on right right right here!

Do you continue to undergo in mind in advance once I knowledgeable you which you couldn't tell what type of catastrophe will strike and even as it'll come? Add to that the reality that you furthermore couldn't tell how it's going to affect you and your circle of relatives. In some instances, it is great to hollow your self in your property and count on the worst to bypass, however there are instances if you have to go away your house and head out into the barren area. In case the latter does take place, you want to apprehend the basics with regards to bushcraft in case you want to truly have a hazard at survival.

Fire craft

Most preppers will commonly have a lighter on them anywhere they pass, regardless if they may be people who smoke or now not, on the way to make a fire whenever they need to. However, you have to now not rely upon these modern-day-day implements too much and examine the primitive techniques of creating a hearth, similar to the hand drill, using a flint, or developing a makeshift lens to harness the strength of the solar.

Before you may begin getting to know about the primitive techniques to start a hearth, you want to recognize a manner to assemble one. First, besides the hearth making tool, you could want to put together your tinder, kindling, and the actual firewood. You can make tinder out of any moderate and dry materials, or you could make some by using way of going for walks the threshold of your knife along the aspect of some high-quality dry softwood. You also can take a few dried leaves after which scrunch them up a chunk to launch the fibers internal.

Once you have got were given tinder, you can start gathering kindling. These are just some small dried twigs, leaves, or something else a good way to effects catch hearth. The reason of the kindling is to nurse the small flame created the usage of the tinder into a few factor big enough to make the firewood burn. Once the fireside is massive enough, you may slowly start consisting of large quantities of firewood into the flames.

Using a primitive hand drill

There are many primitive strategies for making fire, however we can be focusing on the very fundamental hand drill. The first detail you want to do is discover a immediately stick, ideally some detail from a softwood variety, after which spherical off one end.

The subsequent difficulty you will need is softwood fireboard. Look for a flat piece of dried wood after which reduce a small hole, actually large enough for the stick with healthy. Then make a V-customary notch at the edge of the fireboard, the aspect of the V have to connect to the small hole you made earlier.

To use the hand drill, fill the v-normal notch with a few tinder and then vicinity the stick inside the hole. Place each of your fingers along the drill after which rub them backward and forward to spin it. To offer greater friction, press down at the drill at the equal time as spinning it. Continue till you create a massive amount of smoke and a small ember paperwork in the tinder. Tap the ember into a bigger tinder package deal and blow on the smoldering ember until you create a flame.

Here are a couple of pointers on the identical time as the usage of a hand drill. First, make sure that the drill, fireboard, and the tinder are simply dry earlier than you start. Second, in case you cannot appear to make enough friction to make an ember, sprinkle a couple of grains of sand into the hole in the fireboard.

Tracking

It is crucial to analyze monitoring because of the truth you may be the usage of it quite a chunk while you are in a survival state of affairs. For instance, animals should commonly take the same route whenever they traverse via the woods, however you wouldn't see their tracks if you don't understand what to search for. Why do you want to realize about this? For one problem, this could inform you in which you want to stay up for animals while you pass searching, you could additionally use this information so that you recognize in that you want to set your traps and snares. Tracking animals will even provide you with an concept on in which they are getting their water.

Another motive why tracking skills are precious is due to the reality you can use it as a manner of safety. You can tell if different humans, mainly looters, had been snooping round your private home so that you can do the important steps to discourage them from coming any nearer.

Hunting, fishing and foraging

Hunting might be tons a whole lot much less complicated if you had a immoderate-powered rifle with you at the same time as you bugged out of your private home sooner or later of an emergency, however that doesn't normally take location. In most instances, you want to discover ways to hunt the use of primitive weapons, like slingshots or a makeshift bow. Besides reading a manner to are looking for animals, you furthermore may should learn how to hassle dress your kill so that you can clearly consume the red meat. One wrong waft on the identical time as pulling out the coronary coronary heart of an animal can render the beef useless.

Fishing is a lot less complicated than looking, although it takes a good deal greater staying strength and making plans. The essential fishing techniques that you may use at some point of survival conditions are line and hook, and fish trapping. Line and hook fishing technique certainly that, you need to apply a thin piece of cordage with a hook on the alternative stop to snare the fish. You can also join your line to a long stick for added manage, but you can also just roll it up spherical your hands. Trapping alternatively calls for a piece extra making plans. For example, if there's a river nearby, you want to installation the rocks right into a makeshift dam with a small exit. This will funnel all the fish swimming downstream into an searching beforehand to internet or basket.

Besides looking and fishing, you moreover might also want to discover ways to forage for in form to be eaten vegetation and berries. Hunting and fishing journeys aren't always a success, so you need a plan B so that you will although have some detail to consume. You will want to have a look at significantly for this due to the fact many flowers appearance the equal, but now not they all are secure to devour, a few must even kill you brief.

Basic system for bushcraft

Living off the land may be a great deal a good deal much less tough when you have the proper device reachable. Here are the primary gear you may want in case you need to stand a risk to live to inform the tale.

Fixed blade knives

Although there are various varieties of survival knives to be had, it is pleasant to choose out one that has a fixed blade and an entire tang. This approach the blade does now not fold or retract into the address, making them extra stable and much less susceptible to breaking. Full tang technique the metal part of the knife runs all of the way down the deal with, this makes the knife stronger and more difficult, due to this you can even use your knife to cut down small wood.

Yes, Swiss knives and multi-equipment have greater makes use of than a hard and fast blade knife, however furthermore they've quite a few moving additives that cause them to extra liable to breaking. Swiss knives and multi-equipment are extraordinary beneficial for whilst you are camping out for some days, but for survival conditions they're not clearly beneficial.

Hatchet

You'll be the usage of a hatchet for max of the heavy reducing duties that your knife couldn't deal with. Things like slicing down bushes, splitting logs, and dressing and butchering any massive animals that you manipulate to search out. You can also use your hatchet for digging holes and the reverse detail of the blade can be used for hammering stakes and posts into the floor.

When deciding on a hatchet, you want to reflect onconsideration on the device's length, weight and the way it feels to your hand. You must choose a hatchet that isn't too heavy that it's going to slow you down while you're trudging along woody paths, however not too moderate that it does no longer have any electricity at all.

Machete

If you want to have some aspect that has the flexibility of a looking knife with the load and placing electricity of a hatchet then you definately definately definately must sincerely get a machete. These massive bladed knives can actually update searching knives, and they'll be capable of do maximum of the mild art work that hatchets are wished for, so you can say that this one tool is a worth opportunity. Besides slicing down wood and challenge dressing prey, you could additionally use a machete to clean out heavy brush to make it less tough for you and your celebration to journey in even the densest part of the woods.

Chapter 19: Home Security

Most of the time, you do not even need to go away your home in case a catastrophe movements. For example, if the epicenter of the destruction or ruckus is a long way from your own home, the best direction of movement is to stay interior and wait out the disaster that ensues. One issue that you want to be aware of is that in failures and different unfortunate occasions, human beings will panic and lose all experience of decency; there will in fact be greater than a couple of looters who will do something they could sincerely to get their hands in your cautiously stockpiled materials. It is as much as you to shield your own home and your family from anybody who plans to do them harm.

Reinforcing your doorways

The doorways are the primary line of defense of your private home. Unfortunately, the doorways applied in most homes nowadays are made of flimsy substances; a few even use particleboards, which you may in truth punch thru the usage of your naked fists.

The first component you need to exchange, if wanted, is the door itself. Opt for heavy, stable hardwood doorways in preference to the cheap ones that you could discover in most hardware stores. These doors are so tough that it might take a alternatively long term before anybody can smash thru them, no matter the fact that they will be using an awl or any similar implements.

The subsequent things you need to change out are the hinges and locks. It wouldn't be counted variety wide variety if you have a sturdy hardwood door or no longer, if the hinges and locks are sub-par, a great blow alongside those susceptible elements can be enough to knock it down. Replace your vintage hinges with heavy responsibility ones and steady them for your doorways the use of prolonged and sturdy bolts. If you're already planning to update your doorways with stable wood ones, it might be awesome to apply heavy-duty hinges anyway due to the truth the vintage ones you have were given might not be strong sufficient to maintain the weight of the state-of-the-art door.

Besides the locks that include your doorknobs, you need to additionally spend money on a heavy-obligation deadbolt lock or . These varieties of locks are tougher to pick out and are robust sufficient that they couldn't be knocked off their mounting plate without wrecking the whole door first.

Now, in case you're virtually vital approximately securing the doorways of your own home, you need to set up wrought iron doors in the front of your critical doors. This added layer of protection will in reality deter any might-be home invaders or at least motive them to suppose two times approximately raiding your private home for sources and/or harming your own family.

Securing the home home windows

After attempting the doorways, intruders will maximum probable try to gain access via the windows of your property. If you want to strong your property, remove the timber shutter and deploy decorative iron grills rather. Besides together with every other layer of protection, iron grills at the residence home windows can absolutely upload aesthetic rate to your home, if they may be nicely made this is.

Securing the fringe

Once you're completed securing the doors and domestic home windows of your home, the following hassle which you need to consider is securing the edge of your property via putting in a fence. The fence have to be immoderate enough that all of us would possibly genuinely have to interrupt a sweat scaling it; don't installation the ones adorable white picket fences that looters can jump over with out trouble. The great fencing fabric for prepping skills are metallic posts buried at least 3 toes underground, and spanned via heavy gauge cord fencing fabric. If you may, and this is in reality endorsed that you try this, installation razor or barbed cord alongside the pinnacle fringe of the fence to deter people from mountaineering over it.

It is likewise an wonderful idea to put money into an extremely good, independently powered protection system with a view to provide you with a warning of any tries at breaking into your property. You may furthermore need to put more than one booby traps in random places round your home, preferably close to the route critical inside the course of your own home.

Electrifying your fence is also an preference, however it'll now not have an entire lot use if the strength goes out on the same time as the SHTF.

Getting a canine

Dogs are excellent additions for your own family. Not only will puppies love you unconditionally, they will additionally viciously assault all people who may additionally need to dare attempt to harm you and your family. It is usually recommended that you get a large breed of canine to have as your partner, German shepherd dogs, Dobermans, and Siberian Huskies are some of the notable ones for protection purposes. These canine breeds are clean to teach, and they are all reliable to a fault. Dogs can even growl and bark once they revel in that intruders are close by, so in essence you also are getting an effective alarm tool as well.

In any case, simply putting a couple of "Beware of Dog" signs along your perimeter fence have to be sufficient to deter can be looters and raiders from scaling your fence and attacking your private home.

Arming your self and your circle of relatives

Private possession of firearms is a arguable difficulty these days all way to the violent assaults which may be popping in the information every now and then. However, with reference to imparting safety in your own family even as the SHTF (Sh*t Hits the Fan), not anything can beat the preventing strength of firearms.

Shotguns - The issue that makes shotguns first rate weapons is that you don't must purpose them, virtually thing them in the well-known direction of your goal and the lead spray that comes out of the barrel will cope with the rest. You can also use shotguns for searching. If you're looking for a practical, but dependable shotgun, the Remington 870 pump-movement shotgun is the great preference. This precise shotgun is robust enough to prevent any intruder, and it is straightforward to cock and chamber another round in case there may be more than one attacker.

Small-bore rifles – The .22 first-rate rifles fall into this class. The motives why you have to get small-bore rifles is they're pretty silent so that you won't enchantment to each person for your hobby whilst you're looking, they're masses greater correct than shotguns, and their ammunition is dirt cheap so you can stockpile as a number of them as you need. The satisfactory trouble with small bore rifles is they don't have lots in terms of preventing energy, it will take more than one appropriate hits from a .22 excellent if you want to incapacitate an attacker. A exquisite recommendation for a small-bore rifle could be the ever dependable Merlin .22 Auto Loader; this rifle is straightforward to preserve, and correct even for lengthy distances.

Large-bore rifle – This is the huge brother of the preceding gun class. Commonly known as deer rifles, massive-bore rifles are powerful sufficient to take down medium-sized sport from prolonged distances. These rifles % a whole lot more electricity than the small-bores; the ones firearms can use massive ammunition like .243, .30-30, .308, and the ever-famous .30-06. If you're planning to get this kind of rifles, you need to update the scope that came with the gun with an o.E.M, excessive-powered version so that you can release its full capacity. Large bore rifles are high-quality for preventing intruders at a distance; they acquired't be able to get close to sufficient to harm you.

Handguns – People have blended opinions about handguns; loads of them recollect that shotguns are infinitely higher at providing protection. However, handguns are compact, they'll be less difficult to cover and cowl in strategic places in your private home. When selecting handguns, the maximum essential detail which you want to do not forget is the way it feels for your hand. It does not recollect if the gun you personal has all of the modern-day abilities currently available, in case you revel in awkward protecting and aiming the gun then it the whole thing else might probably now not matter range. Choose the gun that feels herbal to your hand, not too slight and not too heavy. As for barrel length, select the gun with the longest barrel that you can efficiently take care of. A longer barrel manner an extended sighting plane, which means snap shots are greater correct. Regarding ammo length, you need to pick out out one that could fireside .380 amazing rounds. In a few states, this is the biggest pleasant handgun that you could cover-deliver.

You also can get an assault rifle, similar to the AR-15, in case you want, however for max people, that masses firepower is overkill. On the other hand, if you count on that you may be trying a excessive-powered automatic weapon to defend your circle of relatives, you've got were given the proper to acquire this. However, for maximum human beings, shotguns and huge-bore rifles are the practical selections due to the fact, besides shielding makes use of, further they have got practical uses. An essential have a look at: in case you do plan to shop for severa guns, make sure that you get proper training on the manner to use them appropriately and responsibly.

These are high-quality a couple of the strategies that you can do to preserve your private home robust in a few unspecified time within the future of worst-case situations. When society starts offevolved crumbling after a primary catastrophe, you cannot depend upon the police and the military to defend you, as they may be most in all likelihood busy a few extraordinary region. It may be all as a lot as you to defend anyone and the entirety that you hold pricey.

Chapter 20: Shtf Survival Tips For Beginners

Shtf survival or this shows at the same time as the doo doo hits the fan survival. Shtf moreover technique the stop of the arena as we realise it (TEOTWAWKI). It is a literal which means that that of world warfare, an economic crumble, a natural mega catastrophe, an invasion of extraterrestrial beings, or a pandemic of thoughts consuming zombies. It is a disaster so that you can effect on all and sundry the which means that of the word "survival of the fittest." Although these devices are too an extended manner fetched, many human beings even though believed that it's far coming. Sometimes it's just a few incidents that display up to you whilst you are to your very personal.

If the cease of days will come, your enjoy and capabilities won't be enough an amazing way to stay on. Shtf survival can let you realize what to do. Preparation is the key to a superb survival. So right here are a few hints on saving your valuable lifestyles:

1.Do not PANIC! Panicking will lead you nowhere. Your cognitive ability might be 0. Everything turns clean on the equal time as you are in a kingdom of panic. If you want to stay on sincerely first stay calm.

2.Think of what you have to do subsequent. Think about a way out a stable hiding location a place to regroup your self. A place in your dreams.

3.Plan a manner to assault returned and live to inform the tale. Gather up substances for one nasty attack on the enemy. Be competitive however although calm. Do not allow feelings like fear guide you thru the manner.

4.Stand up within the the the front immoderate and brilliant. Be the excellent of who you are. Accept the final outcomes. As lengthy as you're despite the fact that alive and surviving. Tell them Shtf survival labored.

SHTF does not commonly suggest the forestall of the sector. Surviving your non-public shtf isn't clean. Preparedness is generally the way to combat of your shtf. If you're underneath such crisis then this shtf survival manual will let you.

What to Do If the SHTF in America

What do you do if the SHTF ("Sewage" Hits The Fan) in America due to an economic crumble, electricity grid failure, terrorist assault or a prime natural disaster? The first element is to realize that most residing Americans have in no way honestly had it very difficult for any period of time, so if there can be an SHTF situation, people will panic.

During the Great Depression 80 years in the past, humans starved to demise in America, but we've got gotten so used to having it so suitable, most human beings expect that in the occasion that they don't have sufficient Christmas affords it is a catastrophe.

If the SHTF occurs, and those are concerned about in which they will get their subsequent meal or how they may save you the strength from getting became off, you may count on them to panic. The frightening detail is that decided humans will do determined matters.

Considering all this, and searching on the training from fantastic monetary collapses and similar SHTF situations in primary countries over the past two decades, it's far smart to consider how you may grow to be organized to make it thru with as little issues as feasible.

The first rule of thumb is that you do NOT want to be in a feature wherein you need to circulate stand in line for dwindling meals substances at the grocery keep. This is even as those who are panicked can come to be crazy Black Friday purchasers at the same time as they may be worried approximately feeding their families.

The fantastic way to avoid being in a capability meals upward thrust up is when you have saved sufficient meals in your pantry to make it some weeks on non-perishables so you can remain very well at home. Generally what takes place is after the initial panic of a catastrophe subsides, people chill out and subjects return to both 'regular' or a 'new ordinary.' Either manner, it's far a whole lot a whole lot much less unstable.

You also can put together yourself by the usage of ensuring that no matter in which you are, 24 hours an afternoon, you cannot be caught on the facet of your pants down. This way that you have a few primary substances stored for your car so that you can 'hunker down' at art work or anyplace you may be until it's miles safe to get home at the equal time because the SHTF in America.

A lot of things must maintain you from getting successfully home on the same time as you want, which incorporates a chemical spill that closes roads or neighborhoods, a strength outage that stops gas stations from pumping gas at the same time as you run out, or civil unrest. Whatever the purpose, you are maximum inclined whilst you are a long way from the protection of your own home wherein your materials are.

How to Survive During SHTF

We now recognise that SHTF stands for "Stuff Hit the Fan," the politer shape, but what does it suggest? Basically, it way Armageddon, the day of reckoning or the Apocalypse. In specific words, that is the time that comes for the worst of all the worst to appear.

If ever it involves skip proper now, what shall you do? Do you believe you studied you can pop out of it all alive? Do you have got were given the center to do what you bought to do? How are you going to live on?

Basically, preparedness is the first issue to be able to boom your probabilities of survival in some unspecified time in the future of SHTF. Have you ever encounter a survivalist? If you do, he is going to will let you recognise to have a stable and properly-stocked safe haven in case of SHTF. True sufficient, many survivalists are prepared.

Among the essential topics which you want to live on in the end of SHTF are meals and water. To stay to inform the story, you want to hold at the least 2.Five liters of water and a couple of,400 calories of food in your safe haven. This is the minimum requirement for a circle of relatives of 4. For effective, this quantity of weight loss program is pretty inadequate. But in times like this, any minimum supply of sustenance is fantastic.

Survival on a lesser quantity of water and food can be exceedingly difficult. A accurate supply of clean ingesting water is almost difficult to discover. And so, your probabilities of getting water are as an alternative constrained. In order to make it via SHTF, storing up water, water filters and purifying drugs is quite recommended.

As hundreds as feasible, fill all easy boxes with water and document them up in the shelter. The disinfected water should be filtered with iodine in preference to chlorine bleach. That is because of the fact chlorine has an destructive effect on the pancreas.

When the stuff hits the fan, it's also very vital to have a super outlook. The catastrophe levels can last up to severa months and commonly have a tendency to take a toll on you. For that purpose, one need to neither get depressed nor determined. This may additionally sound much less complicated said than carried out but try to be greater patient and calm. Being panicky will best makes the hassle worst.

If possible, train properly in advance numerous martial arts strategies. Self safety might be required at any given time which consist of SHTF. Additionally, make certain which you have sun or battery-operated radios further to extra batteries. That way, you hold yourself up to date about the subjects that taking place outside your haven.

The First three Things To Do When SHTF In An Economic Collapse

As a survival professional that specialize in city survival, I frequently inform human beings what to do to prepare for an economic fall apart or other SHTF ("Sewage" Hits The Fan) state of affairs. Unfortunately, most human beings don't deliver via on their accurate intentions to be higher organized.

So what if someone asks me a manner to put together for an monetary crumble and then doesn't take my recommendation?

Well, in preference to rubbing their nose in it, I then inform them what are the number one 3 matters that they should do even as the SHTF and they haven't prepared. At least that way they may have a few information, if no longer resources.

First Thing: Food

The first hassle you want to do if the SHTF in an monetary disintegrate is to make sure a supply of food for a few weeks. Hopefully you could get to the store earlier than all of the crazies are there combating for the closing can of soup or the credit score score card machines no longer paintings. Suspension of monetary organization playing cards can be very not unusual during an financial disintegrate.

Second Thing: Security

After you have got were given food secured, make sure that you could take steps to guard your self, your own family and your own home. If you don't have guns, or maybe in case you do, you will want to have a few way of non-lethal self-safety. Pulling a gun is a big deal and when you have non-lethal techniques of shielding yourself, they are generally higher.

If you can't get mace, go to the hardware store and buy wasp spray. It shoots a circulate 20 feet and may be an powerful deterrent within the route of might-be burglars and looters who would really like to help themselves on your materials.

Third Thing: Water & Power

Expect that once the SHTF, the easy utilities which incorporates water and power turns into plenty an awful lot less dependable. It might not take region in a day or , however it will take location. That has established over and over over again round the area at the same time as such things as an monetary disintegrate display up. Having masses of smooth ingesting water stocked up within the basement is a must.

Finally, make certain an brilliant deliver of flashlights and batteries, because the cutting-edge-day truth can be rolling blackouts and much less dependable electric powered provider.

So now you recognize the first three things you ought to do even as the SHTF in an monetary fall apart. It is as a good deal as you if you can take steps to prepare now or if you can wait until it is too past because of put together and also you need to use the ones steps to truly react and do what you may at the ultimate minute.

Chapter 21: Why Preppers And Survivalists Prefer To Be The 'Gray Man' If The Shtf

A lot of interest inside the community of preppers and survivalists is spent on self-safety and crime and domestic safety, for the motive that we recognize from different worldwide locations which have professional monetary collapse that crime skyrockets.

A term that you may pay interest that describes the fave approach of the extra skilled preppers and survivalists is "Gray Man." This describes the approach of blending in for your historical past and being very unnoticeable.

While the more youthful, extra green preppers and survivalists also can brag approximately their guns, knives and self-protection techniques, it's far a long manner wiser to keep away from a conflict than to want to be in a role to decide out the way to come out on top.

The Gray Man never talks approximately his preps with folks that are out of doors his immediately circle of trusted family and pals. He doesn't want to draw any hobby to himself. While he might also moreover moreover plan to be very generous and percentage additives with others even as the "Sewage Hits The Fan" (SHTF), he's going to ensure that it's far on his phrases. The ultimate element he wishes is a group of people coming to him begging, or worse but, worrying help.

The Gray Man plan isn't actually employed from a "strategic" mind-set, but also a tactical attitude. In everyday encounters after a crisis hits, the Gray Man plans to be very inconspicuous. He in no way wears the best, highly-priced tactical device, as that genuinely attracts attention from the awful guys who're positive to observe and decide that he's a super aim for highly-priced stuff to rob.

In his every day lifestyles, the Gray Man wants to placed on now not something, say now not something and do nothing that might purpose anyone to recall him. This is truely a technique hired through manner of many salesmen who do in-domestic income calls. They might in no way placed on a button for a baby-kisser, as that could flip off humans from the opposing birthday celebration and he dangers losing a sale. Nothing he wears or does or talks about must draw interest to some thing however his product / provider and in addition the profits technique.

When the store clerk leaves the residence, the bulk of the people he has visited shouldn't even remember what he changed into carrying. If they keep in mind that he became wearing $500 alligator shoes, that have become a distraction.

So it isn't handiest that you don't need to position on expensive or tactical clothes in an SHTF state of affairs wherein you are trying to hire the Gray Man person. You don't even need to region on a jersey from a particular soccer group or whatever however bland, unremarkable apparel.

By now not protruding, whether or now not or not in their way of life each day or in how they may make a experience outside their domestic in a hard state of affairs, the preppers and survivalists who hire Gray Man are the least probably to want to fear approximately moving into a sticky scenario.

Items For a Bug Out Bag For SHTF

Ever for the purpose that terror assaults of September 11 we've got were given heard from property like FEMA and all kinds of preppers and survivalists that we need to have a laptop virus out bag prepared in case of a disaster. What precisely is a computer virus out bag and what have to we have were given in a unmarried?

Bugging out way which you need to move away your home on quick be aware due to an emergency. The emergency is probably a hurricane, a chemical spill or natural fuel leak or perhaps an accident at a close-by refinery, manufacturing facility or nuclear plant.

The very nature of bugging out manner you've got were given very little time to reflect onconsideration on what you may need. So, like a pregnant lady who pre-packs her suitcase for her revel in to the hospital, it's far a fantastic idea for every body to each have a bag prepared or no much less than have a tick list prepared so we are capable of p.C. And go away rapid.

The first element to hold in mind is that while you pc virus out and leave your home, if you do now not have a specific, properly perception out plan and a few factors with you, then you definately definately are a direct refugee. A victim is not what you want to be idea of, so plan now what you could do and in which you may flow in case of emergency.

So what are a few gadgets to keep in a malicious program out bag in case there can be an SHTF (Sewage Hits The Fan) state of affairs? As said already, the primary issue is a tick list to ensure that you think about the whole lot nicely earlier, in place of in a panic at the remaining minute.

If you remember instructions of gadgets for a worm out bag as you may thinking about the rooms of your house, you'll be nicely in your way to taking into account the whole thing.

In your bed room, you may suppose of garments and bedding, like a sound asleep bag (and an air bed might be wonderful). In your kitchen, you may be reminded of a few non-perishable food, bottled water and some primary cookware / utensils.

In your relaxation room, you may suppose of private hygiene devices and getting smooth, further to considering your remedy cabinet. The medication cupboard is not to be not noted, because it carries your prescription medicinal drugs, contact lens solution, ibuprofen and unique number one first useful resource objects that you will now not want to overlook.

If you cowl those bases, you will be properly for your way to having a very good malicious program out bag for an SHTF contingency. However, the alternative thing that you need to no longer forget about is a "Get Home Bag." What if a few problem essential happened and also you have been now not able to get domestic for a pair days? That is in which emergency preparedness in your car comes into play.

SHTF Urban Survival Strategies For The Beginning Prepper

For those thinking about becoming a prepper, or as a minimum turning into greater properly organized for a natural disaster, terror assault or a few other disaster, there are a few topics which are glaringly first at the agenda. It's important to preserve first topics first, due to the fact otherwise, a person who is getting to know the way to be a prepper can short get overwhelmed.

Most human beings gaining knowledge of the way to be a prepper make some commonplace errors that come to be costing them quite some coins and numerous time. However, a little training goes an extended way to shortening the mastering curve and supporting you get off on the proper foot.

The first element to do isn't worry loads approximately weapons and ammunition. If you have got the method to defend your self, you then honestly certainly needn't circulate hog-wild searching for all styles of attack rifles and tactical device. Those matters are fun and might thoroughly make us enjoy extra constant, but they will be actually really toys till you've got your priorities straight.

The first precedence must normally be easy consuming water. For a city dweller who has in no manner had a 2nd idea about turning on the tap and consuming to his heart's content material material, this assertion is probably sounding loopy. However, if the strength grid is going down, the pumps on the water plant life will no longer be capable of deliver your tap.

Far more critical than even food, going with out easy eating water for 3 days can spell the forestall of you. And what normally takes place on the town "SHTF" (Sewage Hits the Fan) situations is that when the water goes out, sanitation suffers and cholera can break out.

If you supply in to the temptation to get your water from a neighborhood river or one-of-a-kind ground supply in times like that, you threat cholera, that may actually kill you internal of inside the future with horrendous stomach cramps and "explosive diarrhea."

So, in case you haven't appeared into securing a 2-three week supply of clean consuming water, via every garage or a functionality to purify it, then you definately are losing it slow stockpiling weapons and ammunition. The reason: a person can genuinely take them while you disintegrate.

After water comes meals - and stockpiling pricey freeze-dried survival meals or MRE's is a coins dropping novice mistake. While those food have their vicinity, they must no longer be the mainstay of your food garage plan.

So, there is a lot to have a look at. Begin via way of taking an amazing, hard examine securing a smooth eating water deliver after which flip your attention to meals. Neither of those is as glamorous as guns and camouflage tactical equipment, however they'll keep your existence.

Chapter 22: How To Defend Your Home Against Looters When The Shtf

It's no longer just the folks that watch "Doomsday Preppers" who are worried that the time is coming even as we are able to have civil unrest in our u . S .. More and extra human beings see the handwriting at the wall with our unmanageable national debt and entitlement society and want to be organized for something that can come. The time period "SHTF" (Sewage Hits The Fan) has grow to be a far more well-known time period in this united states for acceptable cause.

Since our domestic is our castle, it's miles herbal to need to revel in consistent in it. Unlike in most one of a kind worldwide locations, wherein every domestic has a wall spherical it and is greater consistent from burglars, our houses within the United States are not very steady. When the police are both beaten or outgunned at some point of a time of civil unrest, having an alarm machine can be little comfort.

Let's take a look at 3 procedures you may make your house extra "hardened" as a capability purpose for rioters or looters or burglars who lose all fear that the police are coming to help you.

1) Make It Look Uninviting

The first rate manner to defend within the route of the "zombie hordes" attacking your own home is to encourage them to move on and by no means even rise up near. This is done with a few smooth steps that provide a fantastic deterrent, without having a moat stocked with alligators around the house.

Having a ornamental wrought iron typhoon door is a first rate way to make the terrible men select every different house, because it's far sincerely more hard to break down. You can also plant rose bushes under every honestly certainly one of your windows to make burglars decide that crawling via thorns is not the pleasant manner to go into your private home.

2) Make It Stronger

In addition to growing your house appear to be a "difficult target" you moreover may need to make it heaps more potent. In the bulk of domestic invasions, the burglar comes right thru the the the front door. If your wrought iron storm door has a lock this is pickable, you then have a problem.

On the alternative hand, if you may't manipulate to pay for a trendy typhoon door, you can make your front door nearly impenetrable while you are home via buying and putting in a "Door Club" for beneath $50.

If you want to secure your home windows, you can reap a movie to have all of your windows covered that makes them shatterproof. Depending upon how a lot you're willing to spend, the film might also want to make your house windows so tough to break that someone with a baseball bat might possibly nearly placed on himself out earlier than the movie-included window gave out.

three) Don't Advertise For Burglars

The worst thing you can do is have NRA bumper stickers for your car and stickers on your the front door marketing how with out a problem you will shoot a domestic invader. While that may be a consolation to you, telling the sector which you aren't afraid, all it absolutely does is tell the horrible men wherein the guns are.

If the lousy men recognize which you have guns, it is able to well deter them from coming even as you are home. However, it can additionally inspire them to stake out your house and pay a visit while you're no longer domestic.

Have a 5 ton gun safe that they lousy guys want to by no means open? No trouble. All they need to do is permit themselves into your property and look forward to you or a loved one to come back decrease lower back domestic and marvel them. The maximum rugged gun steady in the worldwide may be opened very without problem inside the event that they placed a knife or gun to your spouse's throat and ask YOU to open it for them.

The key to staying consistent in your property when the SHTF is a multi-faceted approach. Keep your mouth close to and don't promote it to turn out to be a victim, make your property plenty less of an smooth intention, and harden your doorways and home home windows.

Why You Should Stockpile Food For An Economic Collapse and SHTF

Not satisfactory has the term "SHTF" (Sewage Hits The Fan) entered into the vernacular way to suggests like "The Walking Dead" and "Doomsday Preppers," but greater human beings are surely discussing subjects similar to the possibility of an monetary collapse and whether or not or no longer they ought to stockpile meals.

Let's take a look at the motives which you need to start a food stockpile, more commonly referred to as "Food Storage" for conditions which might be much more likely than a zombie invasion...

The most in all likelihood situation that might befall america in the near destiny is an monetary crumble, because of the fact the debt and the global monetary crises sincerely gained't seem to go away. An financial collapse can be one wherein we have got some exceptional Great Depression like we expert within the 1930's or some difficulty so intense that a reordering of the dollar is wanted.

In each case, the rate of food can be a big problem. If we've hyperinflation, then putting food on the table can be very steeply-priced. If we "simply" have some other Great Depression, then wages will likely lower for anybody and it'll be further hard to give you the cash for food and distinctive necessities.

Since we can see the handwriting on the wall now, with food charges rising faster than in lots of years and the monetary basics of our u . S . At a low thing, it's miles going without pronouncing that meals can be more much less steeply-priced right now than it is going to be day after today.

Buying extra food now and letting it take a seat in our pantry will suggest that, as an investment, it'll without troubles outperform the coins in a economic group account incomes zero.25% interest. That manner that storing up more non-perishable devices, which we recognize we are going to use except, is a no brainer.

You don't ought to be a survivalist or a prepper to look that storing up greater meals to your pantry makes pretty a few experience in easy terms from an monetary attitude. If you be a part of in the belief that the financial fall apart we are going thru may be far worse, then there can be even more reason to stockpile food.

If the economic disintegrate we're going thru is as bad as many experts are awaiting, then meals shortages and food riots are assured to be in our future. In that case, the meals you have saved up ought to store your existence, as it will permit you to live within the safety of your own home at the same time as others are scrambling for the very last cans of soup at the store even as the records breaks.

So you may see that there are accurate motives to stockpile meals for an SHTF scenario like an economic fall apart. The simplest questions is whether or not or not you will preserve considering how you "sincerely have to perform a little aspect" or whether or not you will act.

Bugout Bags And Shelter Plans If You Have To Evacuate When SHTF

If the SHTF (Sewage Hits The Fan) and you want to evacuate, or "pc virus out" from your home, then you definitely at once emerge as what's known as a refugee, and this is NOT what you want to be.

The first precedence for any refugee is to have a roof over their head, and the second to the final location you want to be is in any form of "Shelter" wherein human beings lose manipulate over their each day exercises and can become victimized via predators.

That is the second to the very last vicinity you need to be, with virtually the final place you need to be is out at the streets, uncovered to the elements and virtually without safety from criminals.

So, with that being said, what are some thoughts for steady haven for you and your own family in case you ever should computer virus out?

The first and nice choice is to have prepared beforehand of time with pals and partner and youngsters nicely outdoor of the location in which you live so you can live with them for a time. Many preppers and survivalists take this making plans to the diploma in which they virtually preposition property on the residence of a 'prepping associate' and permit them to do likewise.

This way, every partners have extra peace of mind that within the event that they have to evacuate, they will have garments and other desired personal items anticipating them at a far off place.

Another desire for secure haven in case of a bugout scenario is to have camping tool saved at a storage locker near a favorite campground or state park. Since it might be difficult to capture the whole lot you need within the short time that a bugout generally gives, having belongings prepositioned on this way offers you masses extra flexibility.

By some distance the first-class desire is to have a retreat vicinity properly stocked and away from wherein you live, but this should in no way depend on without a doubt. Due to the man or woman of the emergency that reasons you to should bug out, the roads among you and your retreat might be closed or superb elements need to make it inaccessible.

The number one problem is to have a couple of contingency plan. Any prepper or survivalist clearly really worth his salt knows that Murphy's Law will rear its ugly head and thwart your amazing plan, so a backup is continuously in order.

How To Defend Yourself With Non-Lethal Means When SHTF In An Urban Survival Situation

Even if you're not a "Doomsday Prepper" you need to peer the handwriting at the wall with the monetary device nose diving to the issue wherein topics start to fall apart. When that takes area, the "SHTF"(Sewage Hits The Fan) state of affairs starts offevolved offevolved to spread.

Crime will skyrocket as people's government checks unexpectedly save you or they obtained't purchase a whole lot with inflation turning into hyperinflation and shops will start to ration subjects, worried that tomorrow's price may be tons higher than nowadays's.

This took place to the very wealthy u.S.A. Of Argentina in 2001 and people who write about the lessons that they decided out commonly appear to reputation on crime and personal protection. If we want to be smart and remember an oz. Of prevention, what measures have to we be planning and making ready right now?

Guns? Probably Not

While I'm an avid supporter of the second Amendment, guns aren't always the incredible solution. Certainly if you are in your house and the horrible men pay you a visit, you need to keep pulling the purpose until your gun is empty. But that isn't to mention which you don't want to supply one-of-a-kind approach of protection quick of lethal pressure.

Studies have proven that female cops have a better incidence of taking pictures their firearms than their male contrary numbers. Why? Well, it's because of the reality they have got lots much less bodily force to preserve to undergo in a conflict. This is why pepper spray and tasers have a place, just so an officer who is feeling outmatched doesn't simply have a unmarried desire available in their sidearm.

The identical precept need to be applied to every mother and father. If we've were given satisfactory our brute power after which a firearm to shield ourselves, our options are greatly limited. Now the ones more younger guys inside the "prepper" and "survivalist" moves need to spout off approximately how they'll blow people away for quite much any motive.

However, even supposing there aren't any prison ramifications to killing a person, it's far not often on your exquisite hobby. First off, you want to live with that character's face to your mind for the relaxation of your life. No remember what they did or how horrible they're, there may be a few component difficult-harassed into our souls that values human life: even the existence of a thug.

Second, the person that you shoot and kill nowadays can also have friends who will visit you to pay you once more day after today. Living life looking over your shoulder isn't a first rate manner to live, especially when you have circle of relatives to fear about.

So what is the solution? If you need to apply pressure, you want to have educated and rehearsed the use of the particular stress many, usually. Your reaction want to be drilled into you simply so it is 2d nature, much like the ones within the Armed Forces are knowledgeable.

You need to moreover have a whole lot of protecting technique available to you. Pepper spray is a remarkable stand-off weapon, because it allows you to maintain a bit of a distance. Just ensure to get a amazing gel or some thing that shoots a glide. This gives you extra range and plenty lots much less susceptibility to the wind: you don't need to grow to be getting a whiff of the spray supposed absolutely to your attacker.

An much less pricey, powerful domestic-defense spray is wasp and hornet spray, although in case you shield yourself with it, you're violating the terms of "meant use" imprinted on the can! (please take a look at my sarcasm)

If you want the brilliant spray - splurge with $50 and get "Udap" undergo spray and also you'll get a cloud spraying about 30 toes in the front of you.

I really like sprays, due to the fact knives and stun guns require you to be closer than I'd need to be. The same hassle with the cool, black, ninja-kind collapsible batons - which might be unlawful in some states, take delivery of as right with it or now not.

By a protracted manner the top notch non-deadly technique of self-defense in some unspecified time in the future of an city survival state of affairs is making up your thoughts in advance of time that it is simply your pleasure that tells you no longer to provide your wallet over to a mugger. Nothing for your pockets is in reality well really worth as plenty as your deductible and co-pay for a enjoy to the emergency room after a fight, even in case you pop out on top.

The one of a kind thing to put together for is the very excessive chance that a few civil unrest will break out at the same time as you're faraway from home and, when you have a awesome emergency preparedness package deal deal in your car, you gained't be tempted to try and get domestic right away. The peace of mind that comes from know-how which you have factors for your trunk to get you with the resource of for two or 3 days is valuable.

Lessons Americans Can Learn From Argentina's Economic Collapse for SHTF inside the United States

As America heads toward an economic collapse because of its loopy national debt and runaway spending, we're capable of examine a few awesome instructions about the way to prepare for the SHTF (Sewage Hits The Fan) this is to head returned by way of the usage of the usage of searching at what befell to Argentina

In 2001, Argentina plunged from being a totally rich u . S . A . With a massive center elegance to a rustic wherein the middle elegance all but disappeared. It modified into all because of out of control government spending. Since the scenario is so just like what we've got were given right right here within the United States nowadays, the education decided out are specifically pertinent.

The first lesson to be determined from the financial fall apart in Argentina is that decided people will do determined topics. People took to the streets protesting what they noticed because the theft of the center splendor with the resource of manner of the banks and the betrayal of the politicians. Civil unrest became a common incidence, as folks who saw their economic institution money owed and retirement plans evaporate abruptly had not anything left to lose.

In addition, because the scenario dragged on, increasingly more crime have come to be commonplace. It wasn't simply robberies in awful neighborhoods, however more state-of-the-art burglaries in previously stable neighborhoods as properly. People determined that their homes were being staked out and, whilst all of the people of the own family left and the residence have grow to be vacant for a few hours, they may come home to a house that have been stripped.

In addition, a latest term "specific kidnappings" changed into coined. Instead of truly kidnapping wealthy people where a large ransom may be demanded, thugs commenced out kidnapping people of greater modest manner and disturbing simplest a pair hundred greenbacks. They might stress the spherical in a cab all day till a cellphone name to their home produced some shape of a payoff, after which they could bypass on to the subsequent sufferer.

Express kidnappings had been very clever financially for the awful guys, as the amount of coins taken may also want to now not warrant a huge studies from the overburdened police strain. And within the event that they knew what they were doing, they might pull off a pair of those each day.

Another element that have grow to be not unusual become that former center beauty humans became unlicensed "taxi drivers" the use of their minivans or luxury cars to pressure people to art work or the airport. Others attempted their success to get artwork as a handyman. Women did nails and wiped clean homes. People worked for a fragment of what they used to make, surely in order that they'll feed their own family.

Those searching out economic possibility in a put up-economic crumble society placed that the training (especially vocational studies in which you may educate a change) and counseling professions did nicely, as human beings had to get new talents to artwork and wanted counseling to address a world grew to end up the wrong way up.

Another unfortunate development changed into food shortages and power outages. Although there has been technically enough food for absolutely everyone, in the tumultuous times in which charges must bounce 10% in in line with week for a few gadgets, no grocery stores desired to sell out in their merchandise. Therefore, it have become not unusual for store cabinets to be empty, as an entire lot of inventory have become held in reserve.

Power outages occurred because the utilities and community governments had been strained financially with such a whole lot of people now not capable of pay their payments and taxes. So infrastructure protection and protection were disregarded, main to plenty much less reliable offerings.

There is lots to bear in mind if you need to prepare for an monetary collapse within the United States. The exceptional way to start your "preps" (that could be a time period that preppers use) is with the resource of first studying what has came about earlier than so when records repeats itself, you may be organized rather of having regrets.

Chapter 23: Stockpiling Wheat For Food Shortages When The Shtf

If you've seen the show "Doomsday Preppers" and you would like to stockpile a few food, certainly in case, you can find that you may't sincerely control to pay for a twelve months's supply of food. However, if you check a bit bit about food garage, you'll discover that you could collect a three hundred and sixty five days's deliver loads greater economically that you idea so you will be a prepper yourself.

The key is to stockpile staples, like wheat, in desire to freeze-dried survival components or Army MRE's. The price is an entire lot, an entire lot tons a good deal much less and stocking wheat does plenty greater for you than you will in all likelihood realize. Let's look at the benefits of stocking wheat, and the way it could be used as a cornerstone of your meals storage to hold you and your family alive for a long time.

1) Where To Get Wheat

First off, we aren't speakme about flour right right here. We are talking about the whole wheat kernels, or "wheat berries" as they're stated. Go on-line and you could discover a community LDS Cannery (the "Latter Day Saints" are the Mormon Church) and you can each pick out it up or have it shipped.

Having wheat in #10 cans will provide you with a shelf lifestyles of 20 years or greater. It may be very less luxurious and, unlike flour that has been processed and stripped of nutrients, wheat berries consist of an high-quality quantity of vitamins. Preparing the wheat berries yourself ensures that there are not any preservatives or one-of-a-type chemicals added and you get the complete kernel with all of the nutrients.

2) Wheat Is Versatile

Even in case you're now not a baker, you may consume wheat in hundreds of techniques which can be very smooth to prepare. Soak the wheat berries in a unmarried day and you can eat them as a crunchy cereal. Toast them within the oven for a crunch snack. Put them inside the blender with milk and water and make pancake batter (the healthiest pancake you'll ever consume, and that they flavor excellent).

If you want to growth the amount of nutrients, mainly Vitamin C, then you may both sprout the wheat berries and characteristic salad greens or amplify them into wheat grass, which health food shops positioned into very wholesome smoothies.

There are an entire lot of splendid movies on YouTube, in addition to property from the LDS cannery internet internet site, that will help you take infant steps proper away to get going within the direction of understanding a manner to consist of wheat berries into your weekly menu plan.

That is the crucial thing to prepping. By making small manner of lifestyles adjustments to include such things as meals storage and wheat berries into your each day everyday, even as the SHTF (Sewage Hits The Fan) you received't enjoy similar to the rug has been in reality pulled out from below you. You ought to have saved coins and acquired peace of mind because of the reality you have been smart and took steps to put together in advance of time.

3 Must-Have Skills For Every Prepper Getting Ready For SHTF

You can be an aspiring "Doomsday Prepper" or in all likelihood you're definitely worried about some issue brief of a complete-blown "SHTF" scenario. Either way, you are questioning what you could do, right now, to come to be higher organized for a herbal catastrophe, terror assault or an economic calamity like skyrocketing inflation.

1) Camping? Yes, Camping!

If the electricity is going out and stays out for any period of time, the individuals who will go through the least are those who've enjoy camping. Now allow's be clean proper right here - even as there can be some advantage that can be derived out of your experience "camping" for your $seventy five,000 RV, what we are really speakme approximately proper right here is tent tenting.

The character who's able to "live to tell the tale" without electricity on the identical time as camping over the weekend isn't always going to have a involved breakdown whilst faced with a high electric powered powered strength outage. Don't underestimate the rate of the little matters, like mastering to prepare meals without your Pampered Chef implements or your Cuisinart!

2) Food Storage Skills

Food garage capabilities encompass loads greater than in reality buying a meals stockpile and stacking the packing containers in your basement. It manner which you understand a way to cook from the staples which you have stored up and you achieve this on a normal foundation

Doing this protects you cash, as cooking from scratch is normally much much less expensive than ingesting organized foods or ingesting out, and it furthermore guarantees that you are acquainted with cooking meals out of your meals storage.

3) Networking

Since no prepper can probably hold close all the abilities he desires to shield himself and his family, it's miles critical to make bigger a network of humans which have the competencies you lack. The first-rate way to attract the people you want for your network is to attention on what you need to provide them.

If matters pass south in this u.S. Of america and we're going through an economic crumble or worse, then you may need to realize a person who's a handyman who can repair matters which you don't have a clue approximately. You'll need to have get admission to to a person with a nursing history and a automobile mechanic and a person who's an skilled gardener and a seamstress.

The possibility is to spend a life-time becoming gifted in these types of talents and hoping that not a few factor takes place in the period in-between. However, through supplying what you have got got within the way of capabilities, you'll be capable of help others at the same time as also getting helped yourself.

3 Flashlights Recommendations For Power Outages When The SHTF

Everyone thinks it's an superb idea to have a flashlight in a drawer somewhere, however how a lot of them have actual batteries and what will you certainly preference you had whilst the strength goes out? The truth which you don't ought to be someone from the show "Doomsday Preppers" to realize what a remarkable treatment it's far going to be to have emergency lights even as there may be a blackout.

And you don't ought to be getting geared up for a few "SHTF" (Sewage Hits The Fan) situation - you can really be concerned about a intense storm that takes out the power for some hours.

But even if you realize that your ninety nine cent flashlight with antique batteries isn't enough to maintain in thoughts your self organized, in which do you begin? If you take a look at out the disaster and survival web sites on-line, you'll likely get sticker wonder right away as fast as you see that you can without trouble spend $seventy five on a pocket flashlight.

Not simplest do you need to preserve in thoughts how lots to spend, but what form of lighting fixtures do you need and how many should you have got? Let's have a look at three rules for buying emergency lighting in case the electricity goes out.

1) Lithium Batteries!

No be counted what flashlights you get, you need it to art work and closing prolonged. Lithium batteries fee about twice what everyday batteries fee, however they closing longer and, truely as importantly, they keep a rate well whilst they'll be very cold.

Even if you're now not backpacking within the mountains, you could discover yourself in a situation in which the cold is robbing your batteries of electricity, so that you want lithium. That flashlight is probably ice bloodless in the wintry climate while you leave it within the trunk of your vehicle and you need it to paintings!

2) Go LED

Instead of the conventional lightbulbs, you need LED lights on your flashlight because of the fact they last plenty longer and that they use an entire lot much less energy from the batteries. This manner that the LED slight to your drawer will prove plenty more reliable and also you'll be capable of count on it on the identical time as you want it maximum.

3) Standardize With Three Flashlights

If you've ever tried to do some thing even as maintaining a flashlight on the identical time, you already know the manner demanding it could be. For this purpose, purchase a headlamp much like the backpackers use on your first moderate. You might also moreover look goofy, however you're no longer trying to win any fashion awards.

Having loose arms whilst you're in the darkish looking to get things performed is certainly truely really worth plenty. The headlamp will direct the mild inside the route of whatever you're looking at. It's a exquisite idea NOT to need to examine the lesson the tough manner.

The 2d moderate you should have is a table lantern of some kind so you can use it to mild up the kitchen, rest room or wherever you are. This goals no rationalization.

The 1/3 mild is a backup, pocket-sized flashlight that you may take with you. If your headlamp is going out or in case you want a spare to loan to a person, you'll be happy you have this.

Finally, standardize all three of those lighting round ONE battery kind. I advocate AA batteries. This avoids the hassle of getting to fear approximately stocking three one-of-a-type forms of batteries.

Chapter 24: Three Everyday Carry (Edc) Prepper Items For Your Keychain When The Shtf

You don't have to be a "Doomsday Prepper" to understand that it's miles a brilliant concept to have positive items with you in case of an emergency. Preppers and survivalists name the ones objects their "EDC" (Every Day Carry) objects. Depending on how an extended way you're taking emergency preparedness, your EDC gadgets may moreover fill your pocket, a tactical "guy-bag" or maybe a backpack within the trunk of your vehicle.

Let's test a very modest EDC device that might in shape for your keychain and will show to be a lifesaver if the SHTF (Sewage Hits the Fan) ever happens in America.

Item 1: P-38 Can Opener

This item weighs subsequent to not anything, may be bought at any Army surplus store or outdoors / camping save, and weighs next to not something. It is prepared the scale of a small key, so it acquired't overwhelm your keychain, but if you ever find yourself in a scenario in which you may't get home, it's going to effortlessly open the canned gadgets that every smart prepper need to have within the trunk of his vehicle.

Item 2: Flashlight / Kubotan

Having a small, penlight battery flashlight on your keychain is a have to. If there may be a electricity outage, Murphy's Law states that it's going to take area on the worst possible time, so having a light to your keychain need to definitely are available in on hand.

If you're smart and get an aluminum version, like a exceptional mini-Maglite or a Brinkman slight, then this could double as a Kubotan for self-safety. That is a weapon for near preventing that you use to jab in someone's ribs or neck or (nicely, that's an entire article collection via itself!) to deliver ache or incapacitate an attacker long enough a superb way to escape nicely.

The different hassle that this flashlight can do is break a vehicle window if you are trapped and need to get out (or get in to rescue someone after a crash) in a hurry.

Item three: Leatherman Micra

Okay, a number of the preppers and survivalists will bristle at this idea, as they might already have a splendid multi-tool on their belt initially. However, this is about hints for the top three things I may also bring in my pocket on a keychain, and if you have this base blanketed some distinct manner, all the better.

The first rate thing about a multi-tool like a Leatherman is that it offers you a sharp knife and numerous specific alternatives. Don't underestimate the usefulness of a multi-tool; there are numerous backpacking survivalist sorts who take their Leatherman into the woods with them, and the most vital tool on the big Leathermans is more than one pliers, which many wouldn't bear in mind is probably desired within the woods.

Now with any luck if you don't already have an EDC approach, this could come up with a begin, and you may get these 3 devices for beneath $50 ordinary. The worst element you can do is to begin analyzing and comparing and get into the over assessment that results in paralysis and turn out to be in no manner doing whatever.

The EDC package deal that you have on you whilst disaster moves is infinitely better that the perfect EDC package which you in no manner have been given round to setting together!

Electrical Power Grid Failure: The Most Probably SHTF Scenario

If you need searching the zombies on "The Walking Dead" or the survivalists on "Doomsday Preppers" you have got got probably engaged in a few kind of debate on what's the most in all likelihood "SHTF" (Sewage Hits The Fan) scenario to truly take region in the near destiny.

Since you probable didn't pick out out "zombie apocalypse" as very in all likelihood, it's an superb wager which you concept that a failure of the national energy grid have become excessive on the listing.

The truth is that our developing old electric powered powered power grid infrastructure, mixed with the vulnerability of its internet-installation manage facilities, makes crippling our america of the united states with the aid of having rid of our strength a very attractive preference for terrorists.

It seems that every week we look at about hackers looking for to assault the command and manage centers of the u . S . A .'s energy grid from other global locations.

The reality that fulfillment might throw america lower back into the nineteenth century is a totally sobering idea. It might be far worse for us than it became for humans inside the 19th century, but, due to the reality at least they knew a manner to live without strength. We don't.

The interdependency of the power grid's most critical additives is what makes this situation so real and so risky. On August 14, 2003 about fifty 5 million people within the Northeast had been with out energy while a prime blackout affected humans all through the Northeast United States and a part of Canada.

The offender modified into a laptop hassle, which underscores the reality that a problem "there" will have an effect on human beings "right right here." How possible wouldn't it be for terrorist hackers to get into the power grid's command and control system?

Consider this. In 2010 a computer computer virus known as "Stuxnet" commenced infecting pc structures everywhere in the global, but the aim changed into very particular. The purpose of this bug become to infect enough laptop structures that after it ultimately have been given onto the computer of a scientist who labored within the u . S . A .'s nuclear software program it can in the long run hitch a adventure on a transportable USB pressure into the nuclear facility, wherein it'd harm the uranium centrifuges. It became a success and created quite some harm.

This suggests us that hackers don't even need to get right into a energy plant or possibly at the same continent if you want to harm their goal. If the cause of any terror company or u.S.A. Is the destruction of the USA, the issue of acquiring and detonating enough nuclear warheads to obliterate the usa of the usa versus attacking the electricity grid makes the choice very clean.

The smart person making prepared for the "worst case state of affairs" is probably practical to assume in terms of dwelling without energy.

How to Survive the SHTF Aftermath

You've possibly been taking note of plenty approximately city survival and the severa elements related to it. It may even impact you to join a class or visit a boot camp and get your self a few shape of in depth schooling.

However during this time you continue to don't realise what SHTF in truth method. SHTF stands for shit hits the fan. People who put together themselves for the town survival life and survivalists don't forget that is the stage at the same time as a civilization is undergoing an entire breakdown and there's a number of unrest in all likelihood from threats of civil unrest, a terrorist attack, struggle or a deadly disease.

So you have got been confronted with a SHTF situation and you've no matter the fact that controlled to pull via with remarkable ease. Now that the situation is going decrease returned to normal and you can ought to bypass decrease returned into your private home. But how do you address this SHTF aftermath? Who gives you the assure which you and your own family acquired't even though be affected?

The fact is that it's far despite the fact that focused on your palms to look that not anything takes vicinity to you and your own family. There's a superb way of handling the aftermath as properly. And if that manner is found, you could be rest assured that not something can likely show up to you. Here are a few subjects that you can do to make sure that you existence gets again to everyday after the SHTF:

1.   Before the SHTF, you'll inventory up on now not handiest necessities but moreover "really in case items" if you have

a strong area to perform that. By doing so, you'll be securing your destiny and, as quickly due to the fact the SHTF ends, you'll have a more than everyday inventory of factors that you'll be looking.

2.   Prepare yourself for a warfare and please don't suppose it will likely be smooth as dwelling in the woods and searching animals and having them for dinner. The aftermath may be such that when the bullets and the saved meals are lengthy long gone; you'll be going decrease lower back to the fundamentals similar to our ancestors did centuries earlier than. It's simply now not going to be a cake stroll if that's what you're searching beforehand to it to be.

3.   You have to be self sufficient. Learn the manner to develop your private meals, the manner to make compost and biogas, and so forth. This will assist you emerge as self sufficient and now not rely on others for the fundamental goals of you and your own family.

four. It is said that fifty% of people is probably vain after SHTF. So you want to make sure which you don't capture any infectious sicknesses. You can save you this from occurring to you and your family by the use of keeping your non-public hygiene and keeping off touch with infected mother and father.

Be self sufficient thru the use of gaining knowledge of a way to stay on after the SHTF. There's no alternative for education in metropolis survival. Rest assured that your coins can be properly spent in the end.

www.ingramcontent.com/pod-product-compliance
Lightning Source LLC
La Vergne TN
LVHW022315060326
832902LV00020B/3477